Joe Fisher

A GLASGOW COLLECTION

Essays in honour of Joe Fisher

Edited by
Kevin McCarra and Hamish Whyte

Glasgow City Libraries
1990

ACKNOWLEDGEMENTS

Acknowledgement must go first to Seán Damer whose idea this book was. Thanks for picture research and editorial help to Elizabeth Carmichael of the Glasgow Room, Mitchell Library; and to Enda Ryan also of the Glasgow Room and Alison Gray of Strathclyde Regional Archives for advice and support. And thanks to Joe Fisher himself who unwittingly contributed to his own festschrift by helping many of the contributors with their research.

Illustrations, except where indicated, are from the Glasgow Collection, Mitchell Library.

CONTENTS

CONTRIBUTORS

Simon Berry	journalist, co-editor (with Hamish Whyte) of *Glasgow Observed: A Documentary Anthology* (1987).
Moira Burgess	novelist, short story writer, author of *The Glasgow Novel: A Survey and Bibliography* (1986).
Seán Damer	sociologist, short story writer, author of *Glasgow: Going for a Song* (1990).
Michael Donnelly	formerly assistant to Elspeth King at The People's Palace, author of *Glasgow Stained Glass: a preliminary study* (1981).
Anne Escott	Senior Librarian, Glasgow Collection, Mitchell Library, compiler of *West of Scotland Census Returns and Old Parish Registers* (rev. ed. 1986).
Roy A. Gillespie	Mitchell Librarian 1968-1989.
Cliff Hanley	novelist, journalist, broadcaster, editor of *Glasgow: A Celebration* (1984).
William Hunter	feature writer on the *Glasgow Herald*, editor of *Dear Happy Ghosts: Scenes from the Outram Picture Archive* (1990).
Elspeth King	Curator, The People's Palace, author of *The People's Palace and Glasgow Green* (1985).
Kevin McCarra	Football Correspondent for *Scotland on Sunday*, author of *Scottish Football: A Pictorial History* (1984).
Carl MacDougall	novelist, writer of *The Glasgow Story* column in the *Evening Times*.
Charles McKean	Secretary of the Royal Incorporation of Architects in Scotland, architectural writer, co-author of *Central Glasgow: An Illustrated Architectural Guide* (1989).
Adam McNaughtan	singer and songwriter, recently recorded *Words Words Words* (1988).
Don Martin	Local Studies Librarian, Strathkelvin District, Secretary of LOCSCOT, author of *The Story of Lenzie* (1989).
Charles A. Oakley	former President of Glasgow Chamber of Commerce, Hon. President of Scottish Film Council, author of *The Second City* (4th ed. 1990) and *Those Were the Years* (1983).
Cordelia Oliver	art and drama critic, author of *Joan Eardley RSA* (1988).
George A. Oliver	photographer and motoring historian, author of *Photography and Local History* (1989).
Hamish Whyte	Senior Librarian, Rare Books & Manuscripts, Mitchell Library, editor of *Noise and Smoky Breath: An Illustrated Anthology of Glasgow Poems* (1983).

iv

INTRODUCTION

BUSES ON the local service in Kirkintilloch carry the legend 'Laburnum Grove' on their destination blinds, and have done so for many years, yet few Kirky folk have ever set foot in the street bearing this familiar name. Those who have might tell you that it is a short cul-de-sac of only four council and five privately built houses near the south-western limit of the town, at a location considered by some to be part of Lenzie and by others to be part of Kirkintilloch proper. It lies perched on the edge of 'Lenzie Moss', formerly known as the Mountain Moss, where for centuries the burgesses of Kirkintilloch cut their peats, a privilege accorded them by the ancient charters of the burgh.

This short, unassuming street has a further attribute worthy of notice. The most furtive of glimpses through the window at No. 5 will be sufficient to convey the impression that the occupants here are of singular lifestyle, and possess characteristics which distinguish them from neighbours round about. Books are everywhere! — history, literature, theology, librarianship, science fiction — mostly unjacketed hardbacks, lying higgledy-piggledy on the shelves which seem to line the entire house. It comes then as no surprise to find that the residents of No. 5 — Joe and Molly Fisher — are both librarians. Here they have reared their six children — three boys and three girls — with some apparent success, for all have attained university degree status.

Across the threshold a sense of activity pervades, even though all six fledglings have now flown the nest. The books are clearly in regular use. They show signs of frequent lifting and laying — the very antithesis of the rows of expensively-bound volumes which line armour-fronted bookcases in stately homes, but are never opened, for as much as a fleeting reference, from one century to the next. By the fireside is the chair in which Joe has written up his many and varied projects — research into the life of St John Ogilvie, and into the works of the Annan family of photographers; notes compiled for Oscar Marzaroli's photographs in *Shades of Grey*; design and illustration of commemorative documents in connection with the 75th Anniversary of St Mary's Church in Kirkintilloch, of which Joe has been an elder for a decade; work on a forthcoming, and eagerly anticipated, *Encyclopaedia of Glasgow*. . . .

A glance around No. 5 yields evidence of Joe's many other interests. Astrology — he can readily cast a horoscope. Palaeography — he can decipher mediaeval documents with the best of archivists. Classical music — he has often been known to accompany violin-playing members of the family on keyboard. D.I.Y. — perhaps surprising for one so obviously of a literary and historical bent, Joe is no mean exponent of the hammer and screwdriver (he originally trained as an electrical engineer, at the old Glasgow 'Tech', before coming to library work). Sketching — above all, sketching. Joe carries a sketch-book about with him wherever he goes, as others carry a camera, carefully recording with his pencil the places he visits — Ballantrae, Scarborough, Iona, Ilfracombe, the Fife Coast. He is certainly a gifted amateur artist, though his purpose is not to impress others in any way, but to record the world as he finds it, in a manner which accords him personal satisfaction.

Whatever the circumstances giving rise to it, recent media focus on the museum curatorship of local history has in one important respect been beneficial. It has underlined the great public concern about community history, and in particular the custodianship of community history, at a period when those entrusted with that important duty are under ever-increasing pressures. Their collections are expected to be comprehensive, well-catalogued and maintained, and well-presented. It is taken for granted that they will efficiently service the growing demand for local information, the desire for knowledge of a rapidly receding past, a heritage which is cherished but increasingly elusive.

Library local collections face the same pressures, the same demands, and the same public expectations as museum collections. Joe Fisher, as Librarian of the Mitchell Library's Glasgow Room for 25 years, is only too aware of this. His awareness was already deep-seated in 1980 when he became one of the founders of LOCSCOT, the Scottish Branch of the Library Association Local Studies Group, the purpose of which is to provide a forum for local studies librarians, so that problems can be shared with professional colleagues and mutual support provided. Joe was appointed as LOCSCOT's first secretary, a post he held until 1985, when he succeeded Norma Armstrong of Edinburgh as chairman. For an organisation like LOCSCOT it is most important to have a person of knowledge and stature in charge of professional meetings, and like his worthy predecessor Joe has assumed the role of chairman in a most accomplished manner. His gaunt figure has loomed over meetings, maintaining an ever-benign presence, and imbuing the proceedings with good humour, tempered with a not inconsiderable degree of knowledge and erudition. His sense of fun has often served to set visiting speakers at their ease.

During his five years as chairman he has maintained a first-rate column in *LOCSCOT* magazine, the Group newsletter, providing guidance for colleagues on topics as diverse as standards/guidelines for local studies libraries, the levying of charges for family history enquiries (deep hostility revealed), and pupil investigations for the school standard grade history syllabus. In recent issues his 'chairman's report' has developed into a feature of real character and humour, eagerly anticipated (I would imagine) by members. For example, the Winter 1989 issue provides an irreverent review of the various client groups served by the Local Studies Department, such as:

Dictor invisibilis — on a bad phone line from London in a Sloane Ranger accent someone called Darralee Hipchirchlie (or perhaps, Jarrabie Ibthurdy) requires immediately twelve eight by five glossies illustrating one thousand years of water transport on the Molendinar — anything suitable will do!

The most recent issue has a controversial (and unfashionable) plea for use of the term 'local history' rather than 'local studies', which concept is scornfully summarised as 'a bit of ethnography, a lot of social science, some anthropology tinged with religious institutions, the literary approach combined with a touch of linguistics'. A change back to 'local history' should be preferred, because 'at once our subject takes its rightful place in a logical hierarchy of levels, from family history to Braudel's *longe durée* by way of local, regional and national histories'.

This unwillingness to go along with fashionable trends and terminologies is typical of the man. His admirable regime as Librarian of the Glasgow Room has been essentially practical and pragmatic, reactive and realistic. The workings of the department have been geared to meet real demand across the counter, not airy-fairy notions of what a local studies service should or should not prioritize. Joe's deep involvement with the Glasgow & West of Scotland Family History Society typifies his approach, stemming as it does from a wish to better serve the needs of the large numbers of family historians and genealogists who present themselves at the Glasgow Room counter for advice and assistance. Other local studies librarians might query the motives of family researchers, or question whether much valuable time should be spent in meeting their whims, but for Joe it is essentially a practical matter. In a library context readers are readers, and all must be treated with equal respect.

The traditional approach of the Glasgow Room staff, as upheld and propounded by Joe, has raised a debating point with local studies librarians in the smaller Scottish districts, where a different style is now frequently adopted. Instead of concentrating all resources on answering enquiries in the traditional way, an interactive approach to local aspiration is taken, with librarians moving out into the community, at the most local of levels, seeking help with collection building, providing a range of exhibitions and displays, and encouraging the widest spectrum of local people to identify with their local studies service and derive benefit from its resources. The two approaches are not necessarily incompatible, but both are extremely demanding of manpower, and it remains to be seen whether the big cities like Glasgow will continue to plough a separate furrow from the smaller authorities. In fact, the Glasgow Room has made moves towards the community approach, with, for example, the *Reminiscence Album* project. The department's ability to adapt is one of its strengths. Joe has for some time advocated the use of computers in local studies and, at least in a private capacity, practises what he preaches, bashing away on his trusty Amstrad. Perhaps computer terminals will soon march with the other machines on Level Three in the Mitchell. In the meantime the Glasgow Room continues to set the highest standards, providing the citizenry with a marvellous facility, a window with a panoramic view of the evolving metropolis in all its complexity.

Don Martin

THE CENTRE OF THE EARTH

CLIFF HANLEY

EVEN AS quite a small child, I had been known to read, a wee bit. Words were to be second only in my life to another activity which I couldn't even spell at the time. I wasn't very good on three-letter combinations.

And that is a bit odd, as well. Combinations, indeed? At the time I grew up, and I didn't grow up very far, combinations tended to be coloured pink, with a wee buttoned flap at the back to permit functions which I have long since abandoned, having elevated myself into the bourgeoisie. Only the working classes have bowels.

I well remember, at the age of five, asking my mother how to spell a very common Glasgow phrase. She said it should be written as Ower the dyke. I protested. 'Ower' sounds 'ower'. In the Gallowgate they used a single vowel and not a diphthong.

It took me six years to get to the root of that problem. When I carved my way into the Senior Secondary, and started French lessons, I was deliciously confronted with words like fleur, and chaleur, and realised that the Auld Alliance had given us keelies that magic vowel.

Did brats talk about louping ower the dyke in Springburn or Partick? I did not know. But thank you, Jean Hurll at Eastbank Academy, for clearing my tiny mind of a weird Glasgow puzzle. If I had of went and took German at Eastbank, I should have recognised the letter 'o' with an umlaut forbye. Eur the dyke, Jimmy. Not ower. Eur.

My dear mother was Hebridean, not Glaswegian. I would guess that yon vowel does occur in the Gaelic, but I suspect she was a bit deraciné by the time I arrived.

And what has that to do with Joe Fisher, you may ask? Well, I tend to blether a bit before I get to the point. What this weird city has given me is an unending stream of bafflements. And then, what it has given me is the Mitchell Library, to let me pursue the mysteries.

When I was a wee boy in Sandyhills, I was magnetised by the local library in Wellshot Road. I ate the place. In my teens, I was sucked into Marxism, which promised me that the world would be transformed to perfection at precisely 3.15 pm next Tuesday. Then . . . ah, then. . . .

Skulking round the library I fell across Freud, who was probably groping under a desk for a kosher ham sandwich he had dropped. In a flash, my world opened up.

Society, the ideal society, was not merely about economic inevitability, but

1

about yon other three-letter word; which did seem a lot more fun than the dictatorship of the proletariat. I nearly destroyed the young membership of the Independent Labour Party by dragging them into inhibitions and neuroses and, you know, physical urges and appetites. Like, filth. Oh, magic. See filth?

And what does all that have to do with Joe Fisher?

Simple. I have lived my life as a pursuer of Glasgow's incredible library system. Mr Fisher must have been but a child when I, a fairly juvenile journalist, found the Mitchell.

I was absolutely crazy about this long-legged bird at the time, but she had to share me with the Mitchell. They both blew my tiny mind, and they put up with each other. I got to know one Dunlop, the assistant director, and he dragged me into a very weird Glasgow symposium called Ours Club.

That was, and is, the oldest surviving intellectual rubbish in Scotland. Its real name is the Glasgow Philological and Literary Society. It got its short name because one Friday evening, when a member had to propose the final toast, he couldn't get his drunken tongue round the name and said, 'Aw, tae hell, Ours'.

A very sort of Glesca thing, that.

In the meantime, I was still wed to both the tall lassie and the library. What magic. And I mean both.

A lady from San Francisco came here a year or two ago, hoping to travel to Edinburgh and track down the diaries of Mary Queen of Scots. I phoned some kind of library in the far east, and was advised to go to the Mitchell instead.

We went. It offered us a book copy of the original diaries, written in mediaeval French. I said to Judith that I could actually translate it for her, because I have French, and I'm middle-aged as well. Grace à Dieu, the library lassie found an English Translation and I was able to scoot round to Charing Cross and have many a café royale instead.

That is the Mitchell. Anything can happen, and usually does.

So we get to the Glasgow room. Yes, let us get to the Glasgow room. I myself have some acquaintance with Glasgow. I sometimes get the impression that I have been writing about Glasgow since I left school. Correction, of course. I was obviously exploring Glasgow oddities since I started school, louping eur the dyke to get there.

But what I know about myself is my incurable ignorance. I really enjoy my ignorance. Every day I awake with the delightful knowledge that there is something else to learn today. The horizon of my ignorance stretches farther and farther with every sun that rises.

(It must be sheer hell being God, and getting up every morning knowing everything, past, present and future. So why bother getting up? No problem for me. I am revered, of course, by people who know no better. But I am blissfully higgerant.)

And since I am stuck with Glasgow — not the worst fate on earth — I creep into the Glasgow Room, looking as if I know everything except just one wee bit of dating or whatever.

And that place is, of course, the ultimate magic. What gets me is that a chap there, um, Thingummy, Whatsisname, eh, Pescator? Something like that. Where was I, again? And again and again and again?

Fisher. Joe Fisher. What gets me, is that that man does seem to know everything. Or, and I go back to my juvenile days in journalism, if he doesn't know it, he knows where to find it.

My dear friends, Joe Fisher is just one of the Greats. We shouldn't inflate him too much, because you can't applaud a gink who just does what he enjoys. Selfish beast. He should have spent his life doing something terribly important and painful. He backed away from that serious duty and devoted himself to selfish fun.

Oh, it sticks out a mile. That man has spent his professional career just enjoying himself and enjoying what he did. I am sure the Wee Frees would not approve. Life is meant to be miserable. Fisher never caught on to that.

And the magic thing is that if it was fun for Joe, it was hilarious for us, the baffled searchers after truth and hilarity about this magical city. We search. He knows where we should be searching. He has enriched our lives.

What can I say? Well, like, ta very much, innat. Awright?

The Broomielaw, 1872

Banks & Co. Edinburgh

4

BODY FOUND — GLASGOW DROWNINGS IN THE EARLY 1850s

SIMON BERRY

It is a paradox more apparent than real that a freelance writer generally can't afford to do genuine research. So it was an unprecedented act of faith to spend a whole working week earlier this year reading past copies of the *Glasgow Herald*. My search — fruitless as it subsequently proved — was for a girl named Barbara, who was an enigmatic sweetheart of the Victorian Glasgow writer Alexander Smith.

She died at an early age and was the inspiration of the rather throbbing ballad 'Barbara' which was greatly admired at the time and later appeared in Palgrave's *Golden Treasury*. Smith, who worked for twelve years as a muslin pattern designer (in a building which still stands through a pend off Queen Street), wrote much better poetry — including 'Glasgow' with its now famous line about Noise and Smoky Breath — but it was the more accessible emotion of 'Barbara' that appealed to the general public when he became famous with the publication of *Poems* in 1853:

> But to you I have been faithful, whatsoever good I lacked:
> I loved you, and above my life still hangs that love intact.
> Your love the trembling rainbow, I the reckless cataract —

Was it for this that I was prepared to sacrifice five days' income (not to mention my eyesight) reading miles of microfilm in the Glasgow Room? Partly so, I'm afraid, but also because the identity of Barbara was one of many unsolved mysteries about Alexander Smith's early life in the Calton. Surrounded by the teeming wynds and colourful street life of the old city, as a young man he existed intensely for poetry alone.

How someone from such an unlikely background became a recognised poet and essayist is a mystery I had attempted to explore some years earlier in a full-scale biography; the identity of Barbara was one of many clues that still needed following up. The Barbara episode is referred to by Smith's first biographer Thomas Brisbane, an earnest young Evangelical whom Smith knew from the late 1840s when they were both involved in a debating society which met every Saturday evening at the premises of a French teacher near George Square.

Brisbane's biography *The Early Years of Alexander Smith: A Study for Young Men* is untrustworthy in several respects, mainly, in the wake of his premature death from typhoid, as a consequence of its misguided attempt to portray Smith as a kind of latterday St Francis. The account of Barbara's death, however, seems to have been no figment of Brisbane's imagination. Briefly, it was the rule that at the New Year soirée of the debating society all members had to bring a lady. 'Around this time' Smith had agreed to meet Barbara in the city centre. When she failed to turn up he assumed it was because there had been a choking fog all day.

He only discovered the truth on the following day 'when the mournful intelligence was brought to him that she had been found that morning lying dead in the Glasgow and Paisley Canal. On the afternoon of the previous day, having made a call at the southern extremity of the city, she had endeavoured to reach home the nearest way by going, as she was accustomed to do often, for a short distance by the canal bank — although her friends had advised her not to do so on this occasion; and, in groping her way by the oft-frequented path, she must have fallen in the water' (p. 106).

My immediate callous thought was, What luck. To be robbed of life in such a bizarre fashion while so young (Smith himself was aged about 20 at the time) is surely the stuff of Victorian tabloid journalism. To discover a press account of the incident, then, should be a simple test of persistence. Brisbane's biography places the incident close to a walking tour which the two young men took during the Trades Fair of 1850 and 'Barbara' was first published in November 1852. As the *Herald* appeared two to three times a week during that period, I was presented with a not-too-daunting 350 issues at most to crack the Glasgow poet's mystery heart-throb. No problem for a part-time literary sleuth.

I was swiftly disabused. Like the heroine from some Daphne du Maurier romance my heart beat faster as I first encountered the magic headline *Body Found* and thought Barbara's secret past was mine at last. But unwittingly I had stumbled across a whole new dimension to life and death in mid-Victorian Glasgow. Everyone knows of the horrifying mortality figures for children and adults, through malnutrition, epidemics like cholera, or even violent death (the 1848 Bread Riots which Smith witnessed). But no social historian seems to have considered how extensively the population was pruned by drowning in the River Clyde, its numerous tributaries or nearby canals.

Even if one discounts boating accidents and swimmers getting into difficulties (a common spot was apparently near Stockwell Street bridge where a stream of warm water was disgorged from one of the early steam-driven cotton mills), the figures for those ending up in the water are still significant. Up to 30 cases a year were reported in the *Herald* during my sample period, the majority of them fatal, at a time when the total population was under 400,000. In the heart of the city it appears that terra firma and the broad bosom of the Clyde were all too frequently confused.

As Philip Marlowe might have said, every body has a story to tell. Of course, some fell in by design — for the poor, drowning was the only affordable form of self-destruction — and some by misadventure. In many cases there is a lack of evidence one way or the other, but our early Victorian *Herald* writer didn't stint his readers of a telling detail or two to help them make up their own minds.

On 25 January 1850, for example, a young man 'with long black hair' was found floating near the 'Spring-Boards' at the east end of Glasgow Green. He wore only a striped shirt and old moleskin trousers. Mr Geddes, the Humane Society officer, recovered the body and took it to the House which is still used today by the present part-time officer George Parsonage.

During February and March another half dozen Bodies were Found floating near the city quays, mostly poorly attired, and one came up with the dredger. The Forth and Clyde Canal also made a contribution: on 12 March a man's hat and a bundle containing some bread and a pair of socks were found floating near Blackhill locks; four days later the body of young Jessie Nisbet was fished out of the canal basin and returned to her mother in the Gallowgate.

In mid-May a mini-drama was enacted one Monday morning when a 30-year-old woman plunged into the water near the South Quay. Rescued by a sailor and a policeman in a boat, she was discovered to be intoxicated and charged with wantonly and recklessly throwing herself into the river to the alarm and annoyance of the lieges and breach of the peace. Hauled before the bailie, she was discovered to be the 'notorious Miss Meek' who kept an improper house in Jamaica Street. That same morning she had escaped a fine and had been celebrating ever since. This time she was not so lucky, receiving 60 days in the bridewell and a sermon from the bailie. Clearly this was not Barbara.

On 28 June I was warmer with a Body Found on the Paisley Canal near Port Eglinton, at the top of West Street. But this turned out to be Donald Macpherson, a labourer from the Cowcaddens. At least the body in this case was identified; later in the year there was a succession of those to whom our tireless *Herald* reporter could put no name. These were probably handed over to the Barony Parish and a pauper's grave. One, on 18 October, dressed in the inevitable moleskin outfit, possibly did not even merit that: he was found to have his legs tied together with a handkerchief.

A 15-year-old working for a lawyer was sent to Port Dundas one evening to deliver letters. He was later found in the canal at a point known locally as 'The Clash'. For once the *Herald* was uncharacteristically reticent: 'How he met his distressing fate remains inexplicable, and probably ever will.'

The year 1851 started with a rash of unfortunate people going over the edge. In January alone seven incidents were reported, including one in the Monkland Canal (only possession: a soda water bottle half-full of whisky), two women who in a thick fog fell over the edge of the Broomielaw but were rescued, and a hawker of spectacles and slate pencils who drowned in the Kelvin.

March was little better. A seaman named John McEwan, who was directed to the Rothesay steamer at the Broomielaw, inexplicably missed his way and 'a brief interval afterwards a plunge was heard'. McEwan left a large family. At the end of the month, on a Friday night, 'a respectable individual having been making merry with his friends on the South side of the river' fared better: 'On nearing the harbour he unfortunately mistook his latitude, thinking that he was at Jamaica Street bridge when he was no further East than the ferry boat stairs near West Street. He pushed right onwards and, as a matter of course, plunged over head and ears into the water. This unfortunate circumstance seemed to have awakened him to a perception of the truer state of matters, as he roared for help lustily. Luckily the ferry boat was close at hand, which without much difficulty restored him from his unpleasant position, nothing the worse except for the disagreeable feeling of being thoroughly saturated with Clyde water.' He was also distraught at the loss of a favourite umbrella which he had parted company with during his descent.

There seemed to be no seasonal explanation for the number of drownings. As nights became lighter one might have expected a reduction, and this was so in May and June. But then in August two drownings occurred 'within an hour of each other' at the South Quay, the victims being a workman and a Norwegian crewman. In September a Body 'Dressed in a black shooting coat, striped trousers and otherwise respectably attired' was found on a sandbank at low tide opposite Barclay Curle's yard. Early one Sunday morning in late October a middle-aged man in moleskins went over the edge at the foot of Cheapside Street, Anderston, whilst at about the same time on Glasgow Green a young woman threw herself into the river opposite Nelson's Monument and was swiftly carried away.

In November and December the numbers increased again. The top half of a gent's suit was left on the Spring-Boards and a body was later discovered. Both were claimed by the sister of a young man named James Hendry. It was explained to *Herald* readers: 'He was of weak intellect'. Mrs Ferry, a pauper widow from Bridgeton, dressed in a blue short gown, was also dragged from the river almost opposite the Humane Society House. She had been seen earlier 'very much the worse of drink'.

At the end of November a labourer, carrying empty fish boxes onto the steamer *Mary Jane*, missed his footing and fell in at 4.30 am. His body was not recovered from the freezing water, by grappling hooks (or 'lifehooks'), until two hours later. Such was the state of the weather that on 1 December the High School declared a one-day Skating Holiday. The *Herald* commented somewhat fatalistically: 'It will no doubt be our painful duty as journalists to record, during the next week or two, the sudden deaths of many throughout the country by falling through the brittle and treacherous surface.' Maybe the cold snap didn't last; few such fatalities were reported.

In early December two bodies of young men were recovered, one at the foot of York Street, a busy stretch of the Broomielaw quay, while on the south bank at the foot of West Street a 25-year-old boilermaker was seen staggering towards the ferry steps, 'apparently considerably under the influence of liquor'. Something seems to have caught his foot and he rolled down the steps into the water. His body was recovered an hour later by a constable with a lifehook. December closed with three more accidents, two in the Clyde at York Street. The body of Christian Sterling, a clipper or darner from the Cowcaddens, was recovered from the Monkland Canal near St Rollox.

1852 was ushered in by the *Herald* with numerous reports of Base Coins being circulated, Child Stripping being undertaken for any marketable items of dress, and Diseased Beef being sold in the shops. The New Year also saw an increase in the number of Disorderly Swells whose favourite occupation seemed to be disrupting respectable dance halls; they were fined one guinea each and sent home. My quest for Barbara was now nearing an end but I was no closer to obtaining the incidental details surrounding her death.

On 9 January, it was reported that, whilst running along the canal bank at Port Dundas, a coach painter from Stirling went in head first but his cries attracted attention. Dr Douggan was sent for and 'the necessary restoratives' were applied. Something similar happened to a street scavenger on the Broomielaw who went over the edge still holding his broom. He was rescued by the ferry boat and taken to the police office.

In February an incident on the Broomielaw helped to demonstrate just how steeply the odds were stacked against me. One Wednesday morning a shipping clerk who was standing on the quay at the foot of Macalpine Street, 'was suddenly attacked by a fainting fit. Being at the very edge of the breastwork at the time, he rolled over into the water and would in all probability have perished but for the courage of Mr Murray, sailmaker [of] Windmillcroft, who gallantly leapt in after the poor man and kept him afloat until a boat rendered more effectual relief and conveyed them both to shore. The clerk was instantly conveyed to a doctor's shop in the neighbourhood and, the usual restoratives being applied, he gradually revived. We understand that in the course of his life Mr Murray has been the means of saving no fewer than

14 individuals from drowning.'

Little chance remained of discovering the time, place and manner of Barbara's plunge into the Glasgow and Paisley Canal. One can only deduce that she must have lived in the Pollokshields area as, from Brisbane's account, she often used the towpath as a short cut to Eglinton Street and thence over Glasgow Bridge into the city centre. I had to accept that Barbara was one of a multitude who, whether recorded or not, missed their footing in a moment of fatal inattention.

Only later did I look for some hard figures, the earliest available being in the 1857 *Criminal Returns* of the Glasgow Police. Here, under a table of Sudden Deaths — rather inappropriately, one would have thought — was a short item on drownings for the year:

52 Drowned in the Clyde
24 Drowned in Canals
6 Drowned in Clayholes etc.
2 Drowned in tubs at home

Undoubtedly the extension of the city's quays westwards at this period meant that there was greater access to the river from the streets. From around 1860, according to George Parsonage's book on his father's work for the Glasgow Humane Society, the Society argued for the erection of more barriers. In the 1862 *Criminal Returns* there is evidence that their efforts were having some effect. Drownings in the river had fallen to 35 (by 1867 they had gone down to 14), while in the canals they had fallen to seven (to rise to 16 five years later). These figures, of course, do not record those who were saved from a watery grave — whether in the great waterways of the city or in the bathtub.

George Parsonage's book, incidentally, refers to bodies being left at the Humane Society house on Glasgow Green for claiming up until 1861 when the police took over this responsibility. Many of the accounts in the *Herald* refer to the 'Receiving House' in Ropework Lane, an area behind the Scotia Bar now occupied partly by the new Carrick Quay flats. The place retains a certain morbid hold on the imagination, but I have been unable to discover any more about it.

Who operated this early morgue, if not the Humane Society? Presumably it closed down when facilities were provided at the High Court in Jocelyn Square later in the century. Certainly by the 1850s its surroundings were far from salubrious. The 1852 Post Office Directory shows that near neighbours included a spirit dealer, a tobacco pipe maker, a coalyard and a cotton waste dealer. Whether Barbara's body ever lay there must, however, remain a matter for mere speculation.

As a footnote to Alexander Smith and his drowned sweetheart, I should point out that this episode was not the only one of its type to inspire poetry. William Barton, whose *Poems* were published in 1879,[1] also felt impelled to mourn a death in the Glasgow and Paisley canal, but this time of a young man from Pollokshields, Allan Dixon, who saved a drowning girl before succumbing himself. A short extract is enough to illuminate the details of just how this unnamed girl went in:

'Twas on a dark and dreadful night —
No beaming star did show its light
To guide the traveller on his way
A lonely girl did chance to stray;
She groped her way from left to right,
'Gainst darkness strove with all her might;
But stumbling, trembling did she fall
And slipped into the dread canal.
'Ah me!' she cried. 'O do me save!
Is there no help? Where is the brave?'
But helpless she did cry and rave,
Fast sinking in a watery grave.

She was lucky, but for Barbara and for thousands of others in the teeming Victorian city the watery grave was only a step away. Most drowned unnoticed. The lucky ones like Barbara were remembered at length in verse, while others received an inch or so of print as a Body Found.

1. This was drawn to my attention by Hamish Whyte of the Mitchell Library's Language and Literature Department.

Map by Moira Burgess

THE NOVELISTS' MAP OF GLASGOW

MOIRA BURGESS

THE READER of Glasgow novels may like to pause, when next reading one, and ask himself — or herself — how he knows it's set in Glasgow. Is the setting stated in the first sentence?

It was Glasgow on a Friday night, the city of the stare.[1]

Are the street-names in the novel to be found on a map of Glasgow?

Ebenezer Moir was in a preoccupied condition in his Glassford Street warehouse. He sat in his private room. Its window was the middle one of three (near the corner of Wilson Street) . . .[2]

Is the fictional city given a name — Gowburgh,[3] Glasburgh,[4] the Second City[5] — which, taken together with various other clues, clearly signals Glasgow? Or is it in fact the cumulative effect of these clues — tenements and closemouths, a river dividing the city into north and south, St Mungo, gangs, a Gothic university tower — which persuades the reader that, though no recognisable place-names can be isolated, he is reading about Glasgow?

What to call Glasgow is, arguably, a very minor technical problem in the complex web of decisions which a novelist is making as he begins to write. I would suggest that the author's choice has some significance. By using real place-names he is surely indicating an intention to write *about* Glasgow, depicting place and people with some degree of realism. (Mindful of that other technicality, the avoidance of any possible libel suit, he may of course blur the geographical accuracy of his depiction at some points, as we shall see.) Conversely, by leaving his references vague — 'the city', 'the river' — he is offering himself the opportunity (whether or not he utilises it fully may be another story) to tap into something larger: the idea of the city, the ethos of urban life.

1. William McIlvanney, *The Papers of Tony Veitch* (Hodder and Stoughton, 1983), p. 5.

2. Frederick J. Niven, *Justice of the Peace* (Eveleigh Nash, 1914), p. 9.

3. Robin Jenkins, *Guests of War*, (Macdonald, 1956), *passim*.

4. James Anderson Russell, *The Scorner's Chair* (Loanhead: Macdonald Publishers, 1973), *passim*.

5. James Barke, *Major Operation* (Colins, 1936), *passim*.

Focusing more closely, we can, I think, identify three main methods by which novelists have dealt with the geography of Glasgow; the business, that is, of conducting their readers around the city, providing a background of streets and buildings against which the action or argument of the book can be seen. No doubt, again, such a consideration is totally marginal to literary criticism. This paper, however, has its origin in a hobby of the writer's: going about Glasgow on foot or on top of a bus, spotting the locations where, for instance, Brond pushed the little boy over the bridge,[6] or Eddy Macdonell and his friends walked down from the Pavilion and through Gorbals, talking all the way.[7] It may not be a very academically respectable way to approach Glasgow novels, but it's great fun.

The first method used is, of course, the straightforward one of naming real streets in the right order, and this has a long pedigree. Bailie Nicol Jarvie can be precisely located in his city:

> ... I can win my crowns, and keep my crowns, and count my crowns, wi' ony body in the Saut-Market, or it may be in the Gallowgate.[8]

Martha Spreull, 'a single wumman' in the late 19th century, is accurate on Glasgow geography, and history too:

> When the Professor bodies rowed their goons aboot them, and shifted westward to their fine new College on Gilmorehill, [it was] a sair stoun to me, inasmuch as I couldna tak' up my apartments in George Street and march after them ...[9]

In our own century J. F. Hendry is particularly exact:

> His own street, Laverockhall Street ... lying between Springburn and Provanmill ... Towards the north spread Paddy's Park ... To the south there sprawled the Caledonian Railway Locomotive Works . . . On the western side Sighthill Cemetery ... far to the east, the furnaces and chimneys of the famous Cowlairs Locomotive Works ...[10]

(though there does seem to be one oddity about this, which we'll return to in due course). Further, George Blake in *The Shipbuilders* (1935), James Barke in *Major Operation* (1936) — though he avoids the name Glasgow — Guy

6. Frederic Lindsay, *Brond* (Loanhead: Macdonald Publishers, 1984), p. 8.

7. Edward Gaitens, *Dance of the Apprentices* (Glasgow: William MacLellan, 1948), p. 50-5.

8. Walter Scott, *Rob Roy* (Edinburgh: Constable, 1818), Dent Everyman ed., p. 203.

9. 'Zachary Fleming' [i.e. Henry Johnston], *Martha Spreull* (Glasgow: Wilson and McCormick, 1884), p. 15.

10. J. F. Hendry, *Fernie Brae* (Glasgow: William Maclellan, 1947), p. 37.

McCrone in *Wax Fruit* (1947), and William McIlvanney in *Laidlaw* (1977), all stick, more or less, to the real map; certainly there's enough material of this kind to allow the location-spotter's hobby to develop into a mild addiction.

'More or less,' however, is a necessary qualification, because here and there a fictitious street-name appears among the real ones; usually just a sensible precaution, as we have said. Peter Turnbull's policemen in general patrol accurately named mean streets, even coming indoors from Byres Road to accurately described surroundings:

> The University Cafe smacked of the 1930s; thin benches jutting from the walls, heavy stained wood panelling . . . [A man sat] under a certificate of merit somebody had achieved for ice-cream making . . .[11]

but we can hardly be surprised when the address of his crazed knifeman doesn't appear in the Post Office Directory. (The long-awaited middle-class Glasgow novel of our times, by the way, could profitably be set up a wally close at 13 Highburgh Road, where, as any bus-stop loiterer can confirm, the numbers — because of whose long-forgotten superstition? — go straight from 11 to 15.)

As a digression, the present writer would dearly like to track down an address not specified in George Blake's *The Shipbuilders*, where accurate street-names are otherwise used.

> At the fork of the roads he bore to the right up Argyle Street, and about three hundred yards along turned into the tunnel of an archway running under a lofty tenement. This led him into a dimly-lit yard that ramified in the most surprising ways. . . . It was a veritable hamlet in the heart of Glasgow. . . . The house that Danny approached through the pend and up a short lane was actually the stable and coachman's dwelling of a long-dead nabob . . .[12]

Did this idyllic place really exist? Or is it an amalgam of several Glasgow backwaters encountered by Blake in his journalistic career? (We may think of the 'hidden houses' tracked down by another journalist, James Cowan, at much the same date.[13]) Some day — almost certainly with the help of the Glasgow Room — I hope to find out.

Where an author changes horses in the course of a book — using real names on one page, fictitious names or none at all on another — caution is not always, however, the whole story. We have seen how Frederic Lindsay's

11. Peter Turnbull, *Deep and Crisp and Even* (Collins, 1981), p. 145.

12. George Blake, *The Shipbuilders* (Faber and Faber, 1935), p. 43.

13. James Cowan, *From Glasgow's Treasure Chest* (Glasgow: Craig and Wilson, 1951), p. 184-6 and 268-71.

Brond casually commits murder at an identified Glasgow bridge, in Gibson Street. Later in the same novel, the scene has changed.

> The black stone backs of the tenements reared up like the boundaries of a prison yard . . . The light was dim like a church but the walls smelled of evil and too much poverty. It was a bad church . . . I came out of the front of the close into another street of desolate tenements and walked out of it into a hallucination of green fields. They had demolished streets of buildings and sown the vacant plots with grass. These dazzling plots glowed like jewellery in the vivid light . . .[14]

We are not told where this is. A real place or an imagined one? It doesn't matter. The power of the description brings it before our eyes — more effectively, perhaps, because it isn't named? — and we know that, walking or riding about the city, we are going to come upon it some day, an epitome of Glasgow, the essence of the city caught on a page.

This second method of dealing with geography — exhaustive description, but no names — adds another twist to location-spotting. As well as looking out for Gibson Street, Glassford Street, the Saut-Market, the traveller may be looking for a landscape:

> This particular district was reached from the town by a main road. On your left as you approached it was a public park; on your right, back from the road, was a railway embankment . . . The main road curved round the south end of the park, then entered abruptly into the neighbourhood.[15]

Archie Hind follows this, in *The Dear Green Place*, by describing other areas of Glasgow: his protagonist Mat Craig's childhood home, 'inside one of these loops in the river' (p. 21), and the factory where he works, 'down a long hedged lane, past a farmhouse, and a small water-reservoir' (p. 24). Mat thinks (p. 27): 'Something could be done with this atmosphere, just simply out of the landscape', and Hind has indeed done something remarkable with the landscape of Glasgow. In his hands the non-naming of places is a considered usage, highlighted by the crux passage where he does name names:

> Up Crown Street was a vista of dust and ashes . . . Gles Chu! Glasgow! The dear green place![16]

The omission of street-names, as of the city's name, can give an extra dimension to a piece of Glasgow fiction, taking it a step away from the purely

14. Lindsay *op. cit.*, p. 37-8.
15. Archie Hind, *The Dear Green Place* (Hutchinson, 1966), p. 11.
16. Hind, *op. cit.*, p. 63.

local. A map reference could add nothing to the picture of the identifiable but unnamed flight of steps where Mrs Ross finds her resting-place:

> She was on a terrace above a park . . . She rested against a stone parapet; and beneath her were trees and night-darkened levels of grass, and beneath these the lights of the town streaming away through the darkness to the river and beyond . . . She moved some painful yards to where a broad flight of steps ran down to the lamp-scattered darkness, and lowered herself to one of the steps.[17]

But the story which ends on these steps may serve to introduce the third method of treating Glasgow geography in novels, which is, from the location-spotter's point of view, the most interesting of all. Mrs Ross lives in Shawl Street.

> Her days were lived within an area of a square mile . . . but within this range were all the needs of her existence: the area office of the National Assistance Board, two public libraries, a railway station . . . the police-station, a fish-and-chip shop . . . [18]

And we are told:

> Shawl Street was coming down . . . to make way for Corporation properties where former slum-dwellers would be housed layer upon layer up into the sky . . .[19]

This, with other references, sets the scene in the early 1960s, but no Shawl Street appears on contemporary maps. Yet the area is so precisely delineated that the location-spotter can't resist an attempt at identification. A railway station? (Central Station, we later learn.) *Two* public libraries? Within walking distance of Kelvingrove Park and George Square? A map begins to draw itself in the reader's mind, and on it, somewhere about Anderston or Finnieston as they were before the demolition age of the 60s, Shawl Street appears.

Once he starts trying to match up fictional names for Glasgow streets and districts with real names on the map, the location-spotter is seriously hooked. Glasgow novelists, a subtle and thrawn body of people, have taken delight in renaming their city's features: the fictional map quickly grows. George Blake, in a late novel *The Peacock Palace* (1958), takes us down Byres Road and calls it Cowloan Road. Robin Jenkins places the education offices in *Guests of War* (1956) at 129 Tubb Street. (Consult any Glasgow teacher, or check a map of the city centre between Sauchiehall Street and West Regent Street.)

17. Robert Nicolson, *A Flight of Steps* (Constable, 1966), p. 157.

18. Nicolson, *op. cit.*, p. 14.

19. Nicolson, *op. cit.*, p. 15.

The most sustained, not to say relentless, burst of fictional naming that I know comes in a novel of 1973 which lays its cards on the table immediately:

> One o'clock had bonged from the Gothic tower . . . The Golden Gates were a memorial to five hundred years of university life in Glasburgh.[20]

There's an oddity about these gates in this book (as earlier in Laverockhall Street), but let's accompany the hero from the Golden Gates down Bishop's Way to the Union on the corner of Park Avenue. We walk, via Kirnside Park and Willow Circus (remember the derivation of Sauchiehall?) to the Arneil Reference Library in St Andrew's Street (remember the Halls?). Further developments lead us to King Street, off City Square; to Market Street (remember the derivation of Trongate?); to the ancient burgh of Glenruther across the River Glas; to the large island of Inchmore, with its serrated outline, in the estuary of the Glas — but enough, perhaps, of this.

One caveat should be entered before we gallop off in all directions on the trail of fictitious names. A novel set in the 1930s or even the 1950s may refer with perfect accuracy to streets not to be found in the 1990 A-Z; the explanation being that true cliché, the changing face of Glasgow, whether due to wartime bombing or postwar redevelopment. A researcher is unlikely to trip up on this, but should also remember the name-changing exercise carried out after the incorporation of independent burghs into the city. The list of 'Re-named streets since 1922' in the Post Office Directory of 1931/32 runs to eight pages.

This is relevant in considering the passage already mentioned from Edward Gaitens's *Dance of the Apprentices*. In Chapter Three, set apparently in the winter of 1912/13, Eddy Macdonell and his friends are walking home from the Pavilion, down Renfield Street, into St Vincent Street, through Mitchell Lane into Buchanan Street — a route anyone can follow today. They pass Jail Square, leave the Saltmarket and cross Albert Bridge, all still recognisable on the map. Then:

> Leaving Albert Bridge they turned left into Adelphi Street and swung diagonally right into Rose Street, a long straight dull thoroughfare . . .

> Gowan Street surrounded them, a dreary main street running from east to west of the city . . .

> They wheeled left into Rowanglen Road . . .

> He marched away up South Wellington Street . . .[21]

20. Russell, *op. cit.*, p. 9.
21. Gaitens, *op. cit.*, p. 53-60.

18

After Adelphi Street, these street-names are not found on today's map, and the enthusiastic researcher may conclude that here Gaitens has moved into another mode, placing his fictional Gorbals in the frame of the real one. This isn't quite so. We may fairly decide, following the route on a present-day map, that Gowan Street corresponds to Ballater Street, and wonder whether we have missed some connection in Gaitens's thought. Should Ballater somehow equate to Gowan, as Bath to Tubb and Byres to Cowloan? Or is Gaitens using *gowan*, with its pleasant rural associations, to point up the grim urban streetscape of Ballater Street? Possible, I suppose. However, the Glasgow Post Office Directory for 1912/13 shows no Ballater Street; in its place, a 'main street running from east to west', is Govan Street. The first edition of *Dance of the Apprentices* actually calls the street Govan Street on page 53, before it becomes Gowan Street on page 54; we'll probably never know whether a moment's casual misspelling or a more deliberate decision originally brought about the eventual rather elegantly allusive fictional name.

Rose Street is similarly revealed as today's Florence Street, and South Wellington Street as Lawmoor Street. Rowanglen Road we can, I think, accept as Rutherglen Road for our fictional map of Glasgow.

And there are many more entries to be made. Joanna Bannerman in Catherine Carswell's *Open the Door!* lives in Collessie Street, above Sauchiehall Street,

> . . . at the top of its precipitous, roughly cobbled hill . . . [with] wide, grey views to the south and west . . . [22]

which can only be Hill Street. Bethel Street, site of the school where Percy Phinn's father was janitor, may remind older readers of the Seamen's Bethel, for many years at 249 Paisley Road; persuasive evidence, with other scattered clues, for placing George Friel's *The Boy Who Wanted Peace* (1964) in Kingston. Frederic Lindsay sets *Jill Rips* in the run-down district of Moirhill, where the long Moirhill Road runs from 'suburbs and green fields' to William's Cross; surely this must be Maryhill. We may even fancy that we can trace an unusual street pattern on the map:

> Deacon Street, Carnation Street, Florence Street . . . they make a triangle, with Merse Street lying on top of it and curving back to join Moirhill Road.[23]

But in view of the unsavoury character of these particular streets in the novel, perhaps they had better remain under their prudently supplied aliases.

22. Catherine Carswell, *Open the Door!* (Andrew Melrose, 1920), p. 26.

23. Frederic Lindsay, *Jill Rips* (London: Andre Deutsch, 1987), p. 63.

19

A similar veil is probably meant to be drawn over Cumbie Street, off the Gallowgate ('I suppose that's the way you behave in Cumbie Street . . .'[24]), and possibly over the rumbustious Road, also in an eastern sector ('He came down into the close . . . into the sweetness of cat's pee and cast-off chip paper and Tam Burke's Friday-night vomit . . .'[25]), but the near-historical settings of these passages, in the 1920s and 1950s respectively, together with biographical clues on their authors Clifford Hanley and John McGill, may allow us to point tentatively towards Cubie Street and Parliamentary Road.

There's nothing socially deprived about Evelyn Cowan's Whitefords, reached by another carefully detailed route:

> Abe manoeuvred into the short cut past Glasgow Airport and through the village of Renfrew, cutting round Glen Park to the main road then immediately to the turn-off to the fashionable garden suburb of Whitefords . . .[26]

Only a slight uncertainty (doubtless carefully engineered by the author) as to the road system around Rouken Glen stays the cartographer's hand; Whiteford seems very like Giffnock, but I'd consider Thornliebank or Whitecraigs.

Clifford Hanley is equally precise about Whiteknowes:

> The Haddows lived in a four-apartment downstairs Corporation house in a two-up, two-down block of four houses in Whiteknowes in the north-west of the city. It was one of Glasgow's older housing schemes . . .[27]

Whiteknowes is quite near the Maryhill Road, and, pending inspection of the housing stock, I'd think of Ruchill. Further, characters meet at the corner of Hirta Street, not, of course, on the map. There is a fine array of island names in Milton, but that's probably too far from Maryhill. An option to tempt the location-spotter is Shuna Street in Ruchill.

The most directly signalled code in Glasgow fiction comes, as one might expect, in the work of that great wordsmith George Friel. He begins with description:

> Once [Tordoch] was a lovers' walk on the rural margin of the city. Then it became a waste land of bracken and nettles surrounded by a chemical factory, gasworks, a railway workshop and slaghills. At that point the town council took it over for a slum-clearance scheme . . .[28]

24. Clifford Hanley, *Another Street, Another Dance* (Edinburgh: Mainstream, 1983), p. 12.

25. John McGill, *That Rubens Guy* (Edinburgh: Mainstream, 1990), p. 86.

26. Evelyn Cowan, *Portrait of Alice* (Edinburgh: Canongate, 1976), p. 5.

27. Clifford Hanley, *The Taste of Too Much* (Hutchinson, 1960), p. 22.

28. George Friel, *Mr Alfred M.A.* (Calder and Boyars, 1972), p. 29.

So far, the reader probably has one or two candidates in mind for Tordoch. But Friel proceeds to identify it beyond doubt:

> An amateur etymologist said that the name came from the Gaelic *torran*, a hill or knoll, and *dubh* or *dugh*, signifying dark or gloomy . . .[29]

It's Blackhill; and the discovery, on the real map, of Maxwelton Road where Friel has placed his Ballochmyle Road (think of bonnie lassies) can only add to the pleasure of a good cryptic clue.

Clydend, the setting of Margaret Thomson Davis's *The Breadmakers*, gives us a tricky problem. It is apparently part of Govan:

> The roads of Govan formed the shape of a ladder, with the long straight Govan Road nearest the Clyde and the more pliant Langlands Road further back. The rungs of the ladder joining these two main roads, from Clydend in the south to past Govan Cross, were . . .[30]

and the streets are accurately named one by one, as they were at the setting date, just before the Second World War. Clydend, then, is at the south-western end of Govan.

We proceed to look for the important location Dessie Street, and predictably fail to find it on the map. Where is it, this street of crumbling tenements and shipyard noise? It crosses the Main Road, which is surely Govan Road. The end nearest the river, known locally as Wine Row because of its shebeens, leads to the Clydend Ferry. The other end leads to 'a jungle of side streets and grey-black tenement houses'. Clues and hints abound; we should be able to plant a finger on Dessie Street, but somehow we can't quite. The author has slotted her fictional street into a real landscape with mind-bending effect. (In *A Baby Might be Crying* (1973) the blitz obliterates Dessie Street; for the sake of our sanity, perhaps it's just as well.)

We may note an early reference in *The Breadmakers* to

> . . . the fifteenth century, when Govan itself was barely a village and Clydend had no existence at all . . .[31]

To dismiss this with the remark that Clydend still doesn't exist would be easy, but unfair. Like Whiteknowes, Muirhill, Tordoch, it has been created and it exists.

29. Friel, *op. cit.*, p. 30

30. Margaret Thomson Davis, *The Breadmakers* (Allison and Busby, 1972), p. 10.

31. Davis, *op. cit.*, p. 8.

But on what level of reality? The search for Dessie Street has raised a point which the patient reader will long ago have tried to make: that if we can't square the fictional area with the actual map, it's because the author has adjusted the map. He is writing fiction, after all. He can bend the universe, and he doesn't care. Why should he? Creativity rules.

Writing a Glasgow novel myself, I pictured a half-demolished area, all broken tenements and wasteground, and named it the Claggans. Readers identified it as Gorbals, which was interesting, since in my mind's eye it was Cowcaddens. The library where my character worked was right across the city at Govanhill; when she left work she walked, in my mind, along the broad paths of Victoria Park, which again I had moved half across town without a by-your-leave.[32] It made a convincing enough streetscape (though a City Librarian remarked, all too perceptively, that I'd put a 1950s library into a 1970s Glasgow), but the end result is that we can't enter the Claggans on our fictional city map.

And in fact the map we really want to draw — Glasgow as seen by novelists — is shifting, surreal. The Claggans, somehow, is there. Cowlairs is placed, with a pleasing symmetry, to the east of Laverockhall Street when the real map says west, and the Golden Gates commemorating the quincentenary of Glasgow University (1451-1951) appear in a novel whose setting date is 1934. Up in the north-west, where ordinary maps show Drumchapel, is James Kelman's District of D., which broods over *The Busconductor Hines*. Of course it is Drumchapel, it's even named as such from time to time; but as it recurs again and again in Hines's stream of thought it gathers significance and power.

> The District of D. was bad enough, especially during warmer weather, seeing the green hills faraway . . . Hines knows the place inside out. During the formative years he resided there with his grey but gold family. It is a district where vacancies readily occur in most sections whereas in other sections they always occur . . .[33]

> Yet the District of D. can be fine during colder weather . . . Snow can be really exciting when you live in a place where it lies . . . Great; and always plenty of other kids to play with, it's good, a good place, Drumchapel's a good place.[34]

Finally these disconnected thoughts, memories, hints come together with stunning force:

32. Moira Burgess, *The Day Before Tomorrow* (Collins, 1971), p. 164-5.

33. James Kelman, *The Busconductor Hines* (Edinburgh: Polygon, 1984), p. 94.

34. Kelman, *op. cit.*, p. 102.

Here you have a woman in middle age, then then, a nice looking lassie with mysterious dreams, who has always been enjoying seascapes. She marries a young fellow. They wind up in the District of D. And the first baby is to arrive, then the next two and they are all leaving school and now a grandmother, the eldest son sitting facing one, lighting his cigarette.[35]

The District of D. — cause and effect — won't readily fit on a map.
And so to Alasdair Gray's *Lanark*. The realistic books 1 and 2 present no problem: Riddrie, Blackhill, the Royal Infirmary. In Books 3 and 4 we are in a different world, a different city, called Unthank. Yet the clues point to a city we know. Tenements, tramcars, closes. Broad streets crossing at right-angles; a square full of statues with a tall central pillar; a cathedral facing a necropolis with a gorge between. It's Glasgow all right, but dragged strangely out of shape and time. We're in trouble if we try to enter this city on a map:

> . . . The hillside was a city square. The slanting lamp-standards lighting the scene, the slanting buildings on each side, the slanting spire of the nearby cathedral showed the whole landscape tilted like a board.[36]

To encompass Unthank, and the District of D., and the Claggans, and the 1913 Rose Street, and elusive Dessie Street, demands more than flat paper and ink: a three-dimensional model — maybe four-dimensional — or its computer equivalent? Better, I think, to go back to our original location-spotter, the reader traversing the city with quotations in his — or her — head; seeing against the real streetscapes a protean, intangible appearance, the novelists' map of Glasgow.

35. Kelman, *op. cit.*, p. 131-2.
36. Alasdair Gray, *Lanark* (Edinburgh: Canongate, 1981), p. 555.

Alexander McArthur — from *Daily Record and Mail*
1 November 1935

NO MEAN WRITER? THE CURIOUS CASE OF
ALEXANDER McARTHUR

SEÁN DAMER

No book is more associated with the city of Glasgow than *No Mean City* by Alexander McArthur and H. Kingsley Long.[1] And no book has given rise to so much controversy or generated so many myths. It has become *the* Glasgow book to the extent that early editions of it keep getting stolen from the Glasgow Collection of the Mitchell Library. It is *the* book which non-Glaswegians, particularly English people, will have read about our city — or at least heard of. Its very title, coming as it does from the Bible, is resonant. Paul is speaking: 'I am a Jew of Tarsus in Cilicia, a citizen of no mean city.' (*Acts* 21, 39).

Two of the central myths about the book concern firstly, its circulation, and secondly, its original author, Alexander McArthur, a Gorbals man. It is widely believed that *No Mean City* has sold millions of copies, and that McArthur committed suicide by jumping in the Clyde in remorse for the notoriety Glasgow gained as a result of his book. A typical erroneous statement is contained in Paddy Meehan's book about the Glasgow underworld, where McArthur is described as a 'Gorbals grocer', and it is alleged that the book has sold 'more than seventeen million copies.'[2] My own interest was aroused at a Glasgow Writing Conference in February of this year when a member of the audience asked Moira Burgess if it was true that McArthur had killed himself because he could no longer handle the controversy surrounding his book. Moira replied that she thought that it was true, but that no one seemed to know the details. She did have a note of some local newspaper obituaries of McArthur, and armed with these, I started what was to become a major piece of historical detective work.

Alexander McArthur was born Arthur Alexander McArthur in the Gorbals on 22 July 1901. His father was a maltman, his mother a McAffer by birth; she is believed to have come from Islay. I have not been able to find out the date of his father's death, but it seems to have been well before *No Mean City* was published. As far as I can establish, he, his mother, and his brother James were long-term residents at 141 Waddell Street in the Gorbals. A neighbour in the same close, Mrs Fullagar (née Carson), who was born in 1925, can

1. Alexander McArthur and H. Kingsley Long, *No Mean City* (Longmans, Green, 1935; paperback edition, Corgi, 1957).

2. George Forbes and Paddy Meehan, *Such Bad Company* (Edinburgh: Paul Harris, 1982), p. 73.

remember them well:[3]

> Mrs McArthur — they were Highland. She was very genteel, a very frail lady with grey hair tied back in a bun, and she wore a wee black shawl and a long skirt. But she was very, very quiet. Very quiet spoken and she never bothered with anyone.

She remembers McArthur himself quite distinctly, as a big, well-dressed man:[4]

> SD: How did McArthur dress, can you remember?
>
> Mrs F.: In a three piece suit, I always remember it and a blue and white striped shirt and a dark tie and always a cigarette.
>
> SD: So he was smartly dressed?
>
> Mrs F.: Oh yes. He was big and broad with a big stomach . . . I can remember Alec McArthur as very seldom sober; he drank a lot and I remember him very dark. I wouldn't say swarthy but the memory I have of him he was always smoking, a cigarette was never out of his hand. He always had a good drink in him. That was when he used to stop and speak to us. He would speak to the children at the close and ask them about the school and how were you getting on at school. He was very polite. He still had his Highland brogue. Another thing I remember about him is that I used to see him in that lady's bookshop . . . at the top of Waddell Street and Rutherglen Road, he spent hours in there.

James was an engineer in the Merchant Navy, and Mrs Fullagar's memories of him are of his coming home on leave in his uniform. McArthur went to the Stag pub with Mrs Fullagar's father, William Carson, with whom he was very friendly. As a girl, she can remember McArthur typing:[5]

> Mrs F.: I can remember him typing very well.
>
> SD: Did he do a lot?
>
> Mrs F.: Yes, constantly, he never stopped . . . He did a lot of typing during the night.

Mr Newell of Glasgow worked with McArthur, and can also remember him well:[6]

> He would be about five foot eight inches, stocky-built, good-looking man with a pencil moustache. He didn't take much notice of people, he just walked on and

3. Taped interview with Mrs Fullagar, 17 July 1990.
4. *Ibid.*
5. *Ibid.*
6. Taped interview with Mr Newell, 19 July 1990.

he didn't wave to them or anything like that. As I say he wasn't the friendly type, but he wasn't an off-beat. He seemed to be in a dizzy all the time. He seemed to be writing a book in his mind as he was walking, kind-of-thing. . . . He always reminded me of a Sergeant-Major. He had a very good manner in walking, style of walking, and you would say 'That's somebody'.

These are the only pictures available — so far — of McArthur before *No Mean City* came out in 1935. Contrary to what Paddy Meehan says, McArthur was in fact a baker to trade. Correspondence of his which I have seen said that he had been unemployed since 1929. But as we shall see, this correspondence cannot be totally relied upon. Mrs Fullagar has a vague memory of him working at his trade when she was young:[7]

> Mrs F.: I don't know what happened but I remember him being in the bakery and I remember him coming home but I don't know whether he was sacked for being drunk or whether it was because he was writing the book. I am sure that it was Bilsland's the baker he was working in.

Be this as it may, McArthur was certainly unemployed in 1935 when the book came out. The 'Publisher's Note' to the first (Longman's) edition — not printed in later paperback editions — says:[8]

> In June 1934, Mr Alexander McArthur, writing from an address in the Gorbals, Glasgow, submitted to us two short novels.
>
> Although neither of these was considered suitable for publication, we were greatly struck with their astonishing revelations concerning life in one section of the Empire's second city. Mr McArthur, we were told, had been unemployed for the past five years and had fought the inevitable demoralisation of 'the idle years' (the title of one of his manuscripts) by writing novel after novel — without ever achieving publication — his scene being always the slums of Glasgow and his characters the men and women who shared with himself the tenement houses and the streets.

Longmans decided to try and do something with McArthur's manuscripts. They had a reader, H. Kingsley Long, a highly-experienced professional journalist on *The People*, a serious Sunday newspaper at this time. Long had already 'ghosted' a book for Longmans by a young Englishman who had joined the gangs in the U.S.A., so he had at least some knowledge of the underworld.[9] In a letter to me, Long's daughter, Mrs Prentice, says:[10]

7. Mrs Fullagar, *op. cit.*

8. On p. V of (1) above.

9. James Spenser, *'Limey': An Englishman Joins the Gangs* (Longmans, Green, 1933); with an Introduction by H. Kingsley Long. (In passing, this is a very interesting 'inside' view of New York and Los Angeles gangs in the early 1930s.)

10. Personal communication, Mrs Gillian Prentice, 2 July 1990.

Although my father was a journalist most of his life, at heart he was a creative writer. He had his first short story published in *Punch* when he was 17. Pitmans got him to write a book on 'The Art of the Short Story' which was published in the thirties.

So McArthur's reader was no hack, but a highly literate journalist. He visited McArthur in Glasgow and satisfied himself of the basic veracity of McArthur's observations about life in the Gorbals. They then collaborated on what became *No Mean City*. Mrs Prentice is quite sure that the book was substantially her father's work. This would seem to be borne out by the contract signed by Long and McArthur with Longmans. The Agreement states that Long was to get 75 per cent of the royalties and McArthur 25 per cent.[11] In any event, the original manuscripts of McArthur's two submissions appear to have been lost.

It would seem that the two authors had an idea that *No Mean City* might be a controversial book, for they included an 'Authors' Preface' which appeared in the hardback editions — but *not* in subsequent paperback editions. This is worth quoting in full:

> The Authors wish to state that their novel deals only with one seam in the crowded life of the Empire's Second City. In their view unemployment and overcrowding are primarily responsible for conditions which may be paralleled in all great cities, but which are perhaps, more conspicuous in Glasgow than in any other.
>
> It is only fair to add that no other city is making a more determined effort to re-house and to help its poorer citizens. Nor should it ever be forgotten that Glasgow, with less than a sixth of London's population, carries an equal burden of workless men and women.

This somewhat disingenuous codicil did not prevent a sense of outrage erupting in Glasgow — especially middle-class Glasgow — on the publication of the book in October 1935. It was reviewed in the *Scotsman*, the *Observer*, the *Times Literary Supplement*, the *Spectator*, the Glasgow evening and popular papers inter alia, but if it was done in the *Glasgow Herald*, I cannot find that review. The *Scotsman, TLS*, and *Spectator* reviews are given below to provide an idea of the contemporary critical reaction. While the *Spectator* review is anonymous, the manuscript records of the magazine show that in fact it was written by Edwin Muir, who did a fair amount of such reviewing.[12]

11. From a copy of the original agreement kindly made available to me by Longmans.

12. I am grateful to Dr James Young of the University of Stirling for making this information and review available to me, and to Farquhar McLay for telling Jim of my interest in McArthur in the first place.

'A GLASGOW SLUM'

No Mean City. By Alexander McArthur (Longmans. 7s. 6d.)
Sometimes a 'human document' finds its way into print, forcing itself on public attention by the sheer weight of its sincerity, in spite of literary failings. When such a document has artistic value, too, its importance is doubled. Mr Alexander McArthur, an unemployed worker in a Glasgow slum, with the help of Mr Kingsley Long, a London journalist, has produced such a book in 'No Mean City'.

The main character of 'No Mean City' is a lad called Johnnie Stark, son of a violent father and a downtrodden mother, brought up in a one-room home in the utmost squalor. Johnnie assumes responsibility for his home after the death of his father, and with it many of his father's characteristics: yet there is extreme pathos in his courtship of Lizzie Ramsay, a girl socially his superior, and in their attempts at making a one-room home seemly and beautiful. Lizzie has fallen in love with Johnnie because of his violence, his unchallenged position as 'Razor King' of the Gorbals gang. She makes a deliberate descent to marry him: he attempts a deliberate ascent in marrying her; but his vanity and a spell of unemployment, drag him once more into fights and even into crime, while his failure to make Lizzie a mother humiliates him so severely that he loses all hope after he has served a term of imprisonment and comes home to find her the mother of a child by another man. Side by side with the story of Johnnie is that of his brother Peter, a steady, intelligent young fellow, who wins a good position in a shop and, on his marriage with Isobel, even attains the almost unheard-of-gentility of a 'hoose with a bath'. The accounts of the battles in dance halls and streets, the single-handed duels when a fallen opponent is trampled and pounded and kicked even after he is unconscious, make appalling reading. The home conditions are little less appalling in their frank disregard of normal moral sanctions and their savagery, and such conditions cannot be described without repellent details. But it is impossible to lay down the book with anything but a feeling of pity. There is such a pathetic striving to get out of the slum net, such real team spirit inevitably degenerating into the gang spirit, and such astonishing physical courage and spiritual endurance displayed by the most violent of the characters that they compel admiration even while arousing horror.

Times Literary Supplement, 2 Nov., 1935

NO MEAN CITY

By Alexander McArthur and H. Kingsley Long (7s. 6d. Longmans)
This is an exceedingly sordid novel and it is on account of its very sordidness that it will startle readers. It is the work of an unemployed Glasgow baker who has written it in collaboration with a London journalist. Mr McArthur, who was brought up in the Gorbals district of Glasgow, is well acquainted with the actual living conditions in the slums of the city, and the authors maintain that they have not exaggerated any of the details in their picture. One can readily believe that there would be little temptation to darken still further descriptions which, without departing from reality, are incredibly and appallingly squalid. Most people are familiar with accounts of

the overcrowding, the foul and stagnant atmosphere, the vermin-infested rooms, the dirt and insanitary arrangements that characterise the slums and breed drunkenness, brutality, fierce quarrels and fights, gambling, coarseness, and lustfulness. But here all these things are presented with the peculiar graphical quality of fiction, which shows them in a more vivid light than any straightforward description could do.

No Mean City deals with the career of Johnnie Stark, who wins the title of the Razor King by his prowess in slashing the faces of his opponents. In the gang fights that form a feature of the Glasgow underworld, he takes a leading part attaining a notoriety that makes him envied by all his compeers. This unspeakable ruffian is finally kicked to death in a gang battle, after a career of drinking, fighting, bullying, and loafing. Considered as a novel, *No Mean City* is not particularly distinguished, but from a social point of view it is important owing to the first-hand knowledge of slum life it exhibits. Its view of human nature in a far from attractive manifestation will humiliate the reader, but at the same time it arouses the pity and sympathy one feels for the victims of tragedy. It shows that the slum-dwellers cannot save themselves, but for their own sake and for the sake of society as a whole they must be rescued from their sub-human surroundings.

Scotsman, 31 Oct., 1935

'GLASGOW SLUMS'

No Mean City by Arthur McArthur and H. Kingsley Long. (Longmans 7s. 6d.)
Mr McArthur is a workman who has been out of work for five years. He was born and bred in the Gorbals, a bad and extensive slum in the South Side of Glasgow. This story, in which Mr Kingsley Long has collaborated with him, describes with considerable frankness the life he knows as he has learned of it by experience. There is no reason to question the honesty of his picture, which though appalling is never deliberately sensational.

The main figure in the story is a gangster called the Razor King. A few years ago there were many gangs in Glasgow, some of them with fancy and even literary names; but these have now lost much of their virulence. The most remarkable thing about these gangs was their cult of ingenious savagery, and the variety of dangerous or disfiguring arms that they employed, ranging from razors, safety and other, through steel files two feet long, to the spears of swordfish. They rarely molested anybody but members of rival gangs; but in their fights they were completely ruthless; and Mr McArthur describes a single combat in which the Razor King, having felled his opponent, stamps on his face and crushes in his nose. It is claimed that the subsidiary detail in the book is accurate, though the characters are fictitious. If that is so, there is abundant material in it not only for pity but also for alarm.

This gangster life of Glasgow is not entirely due to the appalling unemployment there, though unemployment has increased and intensified it. The authors consider that 'unemployment and overcrowding are primarily responsible for conditions which may be paralleled in all great cities, but which are, perhaps, more conspicuous in Glasgow than in any other.' The picture of overcrowding in this book is almost more horrible than the picture of cruelty and violence. Single rooms and stairhead lavatories seem to be the rule in the Gorbals; the houses are infested with bugs; there are no baths; and there is no privacy. The young rebel against their environment or try to escape from it: the gangs are doubtless an expression of this rebellion. This book is of great value because it describes from the inside a kind of life which exists not only in Glasgow but in all large manufacturing towns, yet is guessed at by very few people.

The Spectator, 8 Dec., 1935

The Glasgow *Evening Citizen* published a leader on the book on Monday, 28 October 1935, and it would be fair to say that this was typical of the reaction within the city:

'NO MEAN CITY'

The book is an appalling but undoubtedly faithful picture of life amongst the lowest of the low — the corner-boys, the so-called 'gangsters,' the dwellers in the filthiest slums. Naturally, the incidents which the authors describe, and the language which their characters use, are hideous. Nor is there any exaggeration. In fact, the authors have evidently felt compelled to exercise some restraint although, we think, they have gone to the utmost limits of what would be tolerable and permissible in print.

Now, a book of this sort may be justified upon two grounds. Firstly, it may be justified on the ground of artistic merit. That is the justification for some of the great works of Zola, Tolstoy and others. Secondly, it may be justified on the ground that it serves a useful purpose by awakening the public conscience to terrible aspects of society which had hitherto been ignored. We confess, however, that this book does not seem to us to be justified in either of those two grounds. It is not an epic story nor is it an example of unusual literary power. It is quite well written, but it is not a great work of art. On the other hand it does not deal with a social problem concerning which the public conscience has been apathetic. In every city the problems of the slums, and the still more difficult problems of slum dwellers, are only too well known. They engage the attention of politicians of every party and remedial measures are in the forefront of every political programme. The efforts of social workers, of the churches, and of all sorts of welfare organisations, are concentrated upon them; and, in the Press, various aspects of these problems are constantly discussed and brought to the notice of the general public. Therefore we are forced to the conclusion that this book is not likely to have much social value in the sense that the novels of Charles Dickens were valuable.

Unfortunately, it seems to us that the book may positively be harmful. The reputation of our city is undeservedly evil. The wild language and hooligan behaviour of a handful of men who represented certain local constituencies in Parliament after the war, made good 'copy' for newspapers all over the world. People, everywhere, judged Glasgow by some of the men who represented Glasgow in Parliament, and whose wild talk gave the impression that the Clydeside was a hotbed of the most ferocious revolutionaries. It was natural, then, that every little disturbance in this area should be reported throughout the British Press and magnified beyond all reason. A clash between two groups of corner-boys in Maryhill becomes a riot, and the very efforts of social workers in our city are taken as evidence of the savagery of our population! As a result, business people in England and abroad hesitate to invest capital in Glasgow, and even to place orders with Glasgow manufacturers. We ourselves have seen positive evidence that this is so. Glasgow has got a bad name, and Glasgow is suffering because of that bad name; and this book, which is widely noticed in the Press, will tend to confirm the evil reputation of our city. Although the authors do make the point in their preface, people will forget — many people do not realise — that an exactly similar story could have been written about certain parts of London and Liverpool and Manchester and any other great city in the kingdom. The very fidelity of the picture will convince those who have no personal contact with life in the slums of a manufacturing town, that Glasgow must be worse than any other city, for, they will say, surely nothing so horrible can exist anywhere else.

This leader led to a dozen or so 'Letters to the Editor' which were pretty evenly split between those who condemned the book for bringing Glasgow into further disrepute, and those who condemned censorship. This latter referred to the decision by Glasgow Corporation Libraries Committee not to stock *No Mean City*. This was reported on in the *Glasgow Herald*:[13]

GLASGOW NOVEL NOT TO BE PLACED IN LIBRARIES

The Libraries committee of Glasgow Corporation decided yesterday not to place copies of the novel 'No Mean City' in the district libraries of the city. The question was raised by the receipt of requests from readers in eleven districts of the city that the book should be made available in the lending departments of the libraries.

The decision to refuse these applications was taken on a motion by Treasurer Dollan, seconded by Councillor Hector McNeil. Treasurer Dollan held that the book gave an unfair and inaccurate representation of working-class life in Glasgow.

It is interesting to note that the Council was controlled by Labour at this time. The book was also condemned by churchmen. One prominent Glasgow minister said:[14]

Glasgow has been having a pretty bad time at the hands of writers, and this last book is an extremely severe reflection on the position of this great city.

13. *Glasgow Herald* 19 November 1935, p. 9.
14. *Ibid.* 5 November 1935, p. 7.

Another minister said that the events portrayed in *No Mean City* were caused by the demon drink, and that there should be fewer pubs in the Gorbals.[15] The Glasgow *Evening News* carried a report (28 October 1935) that certain Glasgow booksellers were instituting an unofficial boycott of the book. Mr Ross Higgins, an employee of John Smith's, the Glasgow booksellers at the time, told me that while Smith's did not boycott the book, the word came down that it was neither to be displayed nor promoted.[16] But that the book would reach a wide audience in Glasgow despite its condemnation was ensured by the decision of the *Sunday Mail* to serialise it, beginning Sunday, 3 November 1935. Perhaps an assessment of its contemporary impact can be left to veteran Glasgow journalist and author, Jack House:[17]

> The first reaction to 'No Mean City' in Glasgow was one of incredulous amusement. Undoubtedly there were people who took it seriously and were angry, but most Glaswegians I knew had a good laugh.

But this was not the case outside Glasgow, as Mr Newell remembers to this day:[18]

> And then you see when I was in the Services from 1939 to 1945 all I could get from the Englishmen when you spoke to them was 'No Mean City'. I had never read the book. But they had already read the book and down in England they thought it was absolutely appalling. That used to annoy me. They were studying a book which hundreds of people in Glasgow had never read!

It is now impossible to say how many hardback copies of the book were actually sold, nor do the publishers, Longman's, have any record. But the first edition ran to eight impressions between October 1935 and August 1939, and if we say that the usual 2000 copies per impression were printed, then 16,000 copies were in circulation before the war. Again, it is impossible to say how much Long and McArthur got in royalties, but from papers made available to me by Longman's, it seems that including his advance, McArthur received some £50 between publication and June 1936. If this is anything to go by, it is likely that he made a not unreasonable sum of money for the period. Kingsley Long, of course, would have made proportionately more.

In 1956 the paperback rights to *No Mean City* were acquired by Neville Spearman, who printed three impressions. In 1957 they were acquired by Corgi, now a subsidiary of Transworld Publishers. Corgi has printed 27

15. *Ibid.* 6 November 1935, p. 7.

16. Personal communication, Mr Ross Higgins.

17. Personal communication, Mr Jack House.

18. Mr Newell, *op. cit.*

impressions, selling 539,000 copies of the book in all.[19] When it was re-issued in paperback by Neville Spearman, it rapidly went into a second impression. And when it was first issued by Corgi, it sold an astonishing 180,000 copies in four months, 45,000 in Glasgow alone, with considerable contemporary comment in the press. The book remains popular to this day, selling a steady 3000 or so copies annually. These figures alone would make one want to know more about Alexander McArthur.

McArthur was never again to achieve the success of *No Mean City*. The only other thing of his published in his lifetime was a short story, 'Life Renews', which came out in a collection in 1946.[20] In 1969, 22 years after McArthur's death, Corgi published a book called *No Bad Money*, written up from manuscripts of McArthur's by Peter Watts.[21] (I will return to the literary value of these two pieces later.) Watt turns out to have been a highly successful author of Westerns; he published well over a hundred titles under the pseudonym of Matt Chisholm.[22] So whatever one might think of the literary merits of McArthur as an author — and this is hard to judge without the original manuscripts of these two novels — Corgi obviously thought that he had produced enough interesting material to employ an experienced professional writer to rewrite it years after his death. At this juncture I found myself in a blind alley as Peter Watts is also dead. But my curiosity was now well and truly aroused.

From a card index of references to McArthur in newspapers, etc., in the Glasgow Room of the Mitchell Library, I found his obituaries. These were carried in most of the Glasgow newspapers and are basically all the same; they look as if they are taken from a police statement.[23] McArthur was found unconscious on the footpath of the Rutherglen Bridge at 17.30 on 4 September 1947, with his clothes soaking, suggesting that he had been in the River Clyde. He later died in the Glasgow Royal Infirmary of Lysol poisoning.

19. I am grateful to Mr Patrick Jansen-Smith of Transworld for this information.

20. Alexander McArthur, 'Life Renews', in: John Singer, ed., *New Short Stories, 1945-46* (Glasgow: William MacLellan, 1946). I am grateful to Moira Burgess for making this short story available to me.

21. Alexander McArthur and Peter Watts, *No Bad Money* (Corgi, 1969). Again, I am grateful to Moira Burgess for lending me a copy of this book. The Mitchell Library's copy was missing at the time. It has since been replaced.

22. See *Twentieth Century Western Writers* (Macmillan, 1982), pp. 156-60. My thanks to Hamish Whyte for digging up this reference for me — and also the *TLS* review of *No Mean City*.

23. See, for example, the *Evening News* and *Daily Record* of 5 September 1947 and the *Scottish Daily Express* of 6 September 1947.

(Lysol is a powerful disinfectant.) The clear implication is that he had committed suicide. He was identified by a ration-book in his pocket; he had only 1/3d in cash on him. He had lived at 141 Waddell Street for years, but had sold his room-and-kitchen house a few days previously. (This in itself is interesting, as no one *owned* small tenement houses in Glasgow in these days. A reasonable hypothesis is that he bought the house with his royalties to give himself and his mother some security.) His mother had died in March of this year, and his brother was an engineer on the Union Castle ship *Dunnottar Castle*, currently in the Mediterranean. The brother wired that McArthur was under no circumstances to have a pauper's funeral; he would pay the costs of the funeral. But when he was buried, only two people turned up, and they were reporters. Mr Carson, McArthur's neighbour and friend, had by this time moved and learned of the death from the newspapers. The press reports said that McArthur still believed that he could write another best-seller and that a Glasgow lawyer had all his manuscripts, which were to go to the seafaring brother. So there *were* manuscripts. The question was: did they still exist?

My first avenue of enquiry was with William MacLellan the Glasgow publisher, who had published McArthur's short story and whom I noticed had co-published *No Bad Money* with Corgi. I found that Mr MacLellan was still alive and contacted him. He remembered McArthur well. McArthur had frequently called upon him trying to get him to publish his material — short stories, plays and novels. McArthur was a prodigious writer. But in the view of Mr MacLellan and his readers, McArthur's material was unpublishable. It is noteworthy that such well-known local writers as Jack House, Cliff Hanley, Tom Wright, and Maurice Lindsay all read McArthur's work at one time or another, and they have all told me that it was very badly written. All, however, agree that MacArthur had a facility for social observation. Mr MacLellan also thought that he had a good ear for Glasgow dialogue and wrote it well: 'It was so ordinary it was extraordinary.' Shortly before he died, McArthur left four manuscripts with Mr MacLellan. He was good enough to let me read one of these manuscripts, a novel, *Gus McKellar*. I can only say that I concur with the opinions of the earlier readers.

My second line of enquiry was to read a March 1947 article in *The Word*, Guy Aldred's Glasgow Anarchist newspaper, mentioned in the Glasgow Room's card-index. This proved most interesting. In this article McArthur accused Robert McLeish of plagiarising his play *The Gorbals Story* from an earlier play of his own entitled *The Mystery of Gorbals Terrace*. McArthur had submitted this play to Unity Theatre in October 1945 after it had been rejected by the Citizens' Theatre. Apparently, Robert Mitchell of Unity had passed the manuscript to McLeish to read — and McArthur never saw it again. He called on Mitchell in March 1946, but did not see him and got no satisfaction. *The Gorbals Story* was first produced in August 1946, and then ran in Glasgow from 2 September to 5 October in the Queen's Theatre in Glasgow.[24] As is well known, it had great success, not only in Glasgow, but elsewhere in Scotland, and England, including a couple of seasons in London. It was generally well-reviewed, but was the subject of a well-observed, highly critical review by Edward Gaitens in the *Scots Theatre* of November 1946.[25] *The Word* notes that McArthur complained about this alleged plagiarism — a very serious offence to a writer — to a variety of authorities. The matter was finally resolved, albeit not to McArthur's satisfaction, by a firm of local solicitors adjudicating the issue by reading both manuscripts. On 31 August 1946 they issued their judgment: 'Neither in dialogue, incident, or dramatic situation was there what seemed to be any point of identity or even similarity to your play.'[26] McArthur was not amused. *The Word* printed the setting, timing, and dramatis personae of the two plays; there is a distinct similarity. It said: 'The question arises: If Mr McArthur had not submitted his 'Mystery of Gorbals Terrace' would there have been a 'Gorbals Story'? Is this not a fair question to ask in face of the similarities in the plays?'

I sought an answer from Linda Mackenney, who edited the book on *The Gorbals Story*. She told me that a manuscript of McArthur's *The Mystery of Gorbals Terrace* existed in the National Library of Scotland, that she had compared this with *The Gorbals Story*, and that she felt that no plagiarism had taken place.[27] She felt further that given Unity Theatre's commitment to working-class theatre something like *The Gorbals Story* would have appeared in any event. So I went to Edinburgh and read McArthur's manuscript myself. I have to say that I do not totally agree with Linda. While there is demonstrably no plagiarism of dialogue or incident, there is equally demonstrably a striking similarity between the setting, the timing, and the number of players. My own conclusion is that McArthur's play detonated the idea for a Gorbals play in McLeish's head. Had he not submitted his play to Unity Theatre there would

24. Linda Mackenney ed., *The Gorbals Story by Robert McLeish* (Edinburgh: 7:84 Publications, 1985), p. 10.

25. Edward Gaitens, 'Gorbals Hoary'. *Scots Theatre*, No. 3, November 1946. In her book Linda Mackenney notes that McLeish's family objected to her printing this review as it was believed to have been motivated by malice. But in fact, Gaitens's critical comments are in line with other measured, critical reviews published in the book. Quite simply, *The Gorbals Story* is not great theatre.

26. 'A Gorbals Story'. *The Word*, March 1947, p. 88.

27. Personal communication, Linda Mackenney.

have been no *Gorbals Story*, in my view. So McArthur had every right to feel aggrieved — and exceptionally aggrieved he was, as can be seen by the many pencilled comments on his manuscript in the National Library.

My third line of enquiry was through the publishers. I eventually was given the names and addresses of the two people who now get the royalties from *No Mean City*. These were Kingsley Long's daughter, Mrs Prentice, mentioned above, and Mrs Wood. Mrs Wood had been willed the royalties by a James Milligan, who was Alexander McArthur's half-brother. Mr Milligan had been left the royalties by James McArthur, Alexander's brother. Milligan was the Session Clerk at Bridgeton Cross Church, Landressy Street, and according to Mrs Wood, had kept his relationship to McArthur, and the fact that he received the royalties from the book, very quiet. He also had told Mrs Wood that Alexander McArthur had been elated with the success of *No Mean City* and was a heavy drinker. The problem is that Mrs Wood has no knowledge of how Mr Milligan came to be the half-brother of Alexander and James McArthur, and Mrs Fullagar, their neighbour, has never heard of him. So for the moment at least, the Milligan connection remains an enigma. Mrs Wood was a neighbour and friend of the Milligans, who lived in Duke Street, and indeed looked after Mr Milligan in his old age. This was why she was willed the royalties.

Much more important is the fact that she was also willed a number of McArthur's manuscripts; these are detailed in the bibliography below. Mrs Wood was good enough to let me examine these manuscripts. They contain the original manuscript of *No Bad Money*, a copy of the play *The Mystery of Gorbals Terrace*, six short stories — and a file of McArthur's letters about the plagiarism issue. This file contains letters to every newspaper in Glasgow, to the Citizens' and Unity Theatres, to William MacLellan, to Guy Aldred, to the Lord Chamberlain, to the Secretary of State for Scotland, to the Lord Provost of Glasgow, to the Arts Council, to Seán O'Casey, to the Chief Constable, and to James Bridie, among others. They run from September 1944 to March 1947, and are heavily annotated. They seem to me to demonstrate an unhealthy obsession with the issue of the plagiarism of his play, and a mind which is becoming increasingly unhinged. He makes accusations about homosexuality which are probably libellous. This squares with the observations of Jack House in a letter he sent me about McArthur:[28]

---

28. Jack House, *op. cit.*

I can't remember which of the three Glasgow evening papers I was working for at the time, but he was a regular caller. He would hand over a batch of his latest effusions, always written by hand and full of grammatical and other errors. They were totally unsuitable for publication. At the same time you could see that he had a strong sense of observance . . . he traipsed round the newspaper offices and was always turned down. He said that was because Jack House, George Blake and most of Glasgow's top journalists were homosexual and, apparently, homosexuals are incapable of recognising genius when they see it.

The letters stop in March 1947; that was the month his mother died. Given that they had lived together for 46 years, this cannot have helped McArthur's state of mind. Jack House again takes up the story:[29]

> The time came when McArthur was completely disillusioned. He had just received a royalty payment for 'No Mean City' and he decided to splash it out and then, appropriately, drown himself in the Clyde. He asked a dozen or so of his Gorbals friends to dinner in the Grosvenor Restaurant in Gordon Street, one of the best restaurants in town at that time. They met in a private room and had a grand meal with champagne and lashings of whisky. McArthur said good night to his friends and walked down to the banks of the Clyde. He had a bottle of lysol in his coat pocket. His plan was to swallow the lysol, then throw himself in the river. He climbed over the railings and went across the grass and sat down to drink the lysol. He swallowed a mouthful and the champagne came up and he was violently sick. He never made the river and was discovered unconscious by two policemen on the beat. He was taken to hospital where he died.

While there are one or two details here which appear to be deductions rather than fact — e.g. how did Jack know McArthur intended to *drown* himself? — I have little doubt that this account is the nearest to the truth we are likely to get. Jack House is the doyen of Glasgow journalists, has a reputation for accuracy, and is not a malicious person. While I have been unable to trace anyone who was at that final party, I have no reason to doubt that it did occur. And McArthur's intention to kill himself was palpable; why else would he have sold his house a few days previously? At the end of the day, one can only feel pity for the poor man; nobody deserves to die like that.

What then are we to make of Alexander McArthur as a writer? What follows is my own opinion, based on a reading of his three published pieces plus his manuscript plays, short stories and a novel. McArthur was plainly an autodidact who read voraciously — his letters mention many great writers, including Ibsen, O'Casey, Joyce, Conrad and Maugham. His two published novels display a great deal of most interesting social observation. In her bibliography of the Glasgow novel, Moira Burgess makes the following

29. *Ibid.*

observation about *No Bad Money*:[30] 'An essay in sensationalism, lacking either accuracy or social comment.'

For once, I disagree with Moira. To me this book is a fascinating if flawed insight into the world of a brothel-keeper in the Glasgow of the 1930s and 1940s, with much interesting criminological detail about police corruption, the organisation of prostitution, protection rackets and gang warfare. For my money, it is infinitely better than *No Mean City*. One cannot help escaping the conclusion that the main character, Bob Leyland — as with John Stark in *No Mean City* — is based on an actual person, along with some of the minor characters. And there are many incidents — like a prostitute 'streaking' naked out of a pub upstairs into a tenement house — which have the ring of truth about them. Further, McArthur very definitely had an excellent ear for Glasgow speech; his dialogue is more than credible. The problem is that he could not write. Criminology, no matter how good, is not creative writing. His prose is leaden, his plots unimaginative, and his characterisation is never far from caricature. His published short story, 'Life Renews', is a case in point. He has many irritating mannerisms, such as giving his characters very un-Glaswegian names. And he had a fetish for the colour green in women's clothes; the number of green frocks and dresses etc. in *No Bad Money* is quite unbelievable. And in his discussion of sex there is something I cannot quite put my finger on, but it has to do with basic credibility. I have a strong *feeling* that McArthur did not have much, if any, sexual experience. One gets the feeling that he is repeating things he heard in the Stag pub in Waddell Street.

There is no doubt that McArthur was driven by a passion to write about the plain people of Glasgow. That is to be applauded. And he had a theme which runs through a lot of his work: working-class respectability, and how you get it and keep it. The manuscript novel which Mr MacLellan has, *Gus McKellar*, is an account of the rise of a baker to the position of foreman. It is almost certainly autobiographical; the details of the processes of baking are too accurate technically for it to be anything else. Yet Gus McKellar, the hero portrayed by McArthur, is strangely unsympathetic, a snob and a parasite upon women. He loves the warmth and solidarity of working-class culture but despises the 'proletarian' (sic). McArthur's theme, the costs of social mobility out of the working-class, is an important one, but he just does not deliver the goods. He is far too intent on blinding us with detail to show us anything interesting. In short, he has no sense of the dramatic. Perhaps the best way to evaluate McArthur's work is to compare it with contemporary writing on similar themes. The writer who obviously springs to mind is

30. Moira Burgess, *The Glasgow Novel: A Survey and Bibliography*, 2nd Edition (Scottish Library Association & Glasgow District Libraries, 1986), p. 86.

Edward Gaitens. There is simply no comparison; Gaitens could *write*.

But it would be wrong to be too harsh on McArthur. In many senses, he was bound to be unsuccessful. Working-class writers have many difficulties to face. It seems that McArthur did not have any literary friends who could help him with fraternal criticism of his writing. Gaitens had Bridie, at least. Consequently, his work did not improve. McArthur must have been given comments by the many readers who looked at his work, but if so, he seems to have been unable to take them on board. Perhaps his success with *No Mean City* turned his head — and the success of that book is really Kingsley Long's. Several contemporaries believe this to be the case, notably Jack House. After this book, McArthur was still *in* the working-class of the Gorbals, but in a curious sense, no longer *of* it. He seems to have had no connection with the working-class movement any more than with fellow-writers. McArthur wrote an article in a local newspaper in 1935 called: 'Why I Wrote "No Mean City".' It is not very coherent. In it he says:[31]

> Working-class people are now becoming 'slum-conscious'. This book ought to add to their number and to their slum-consciousness.
>
> I have never been in any working-class 'labour' party, though I know what it is to labour through the day and through the night; so that it must not be understood that I mean 'class conscious' when I mention 'slum conscious'.

And:

> . . . I just *had* to write 'No Mean City'. The knowledge that unknown men and women had lived lives and died deaths of a sordid kind added to my belief that they did not do so in vain.

McArthur was effectively in a cultural no-man's-land. But he ploughed his lonely furrow, trying to produce his masterpiece, and one can have nothing but respect for his dedication. The appearance of McLeish's *The Gorbals Story* and its success seem to have driven McArthur into a world of disillusion and paranoia; it was to be a world from which he would never return.

POSTSCRIPT

The *No Mean City* saga looks like it will run and run. We have not only had the recent, controversial 7:84 stage production, but there is the possibility of a film. In talking with Mr John Bettany of Headman Productions, who own the film rights, he told me that he was interested in making a television trilogy — three half-hour episodes — out of the book, to be written by a major Scottish

---

31. Alexander McArthur, 'Why I Wrote "No Mean City".' *Daily Record and Mail*, 1 November 1935.

writer. This film would play down Johnnie Stark and play up his brother and the women, and show how different people took different routes to survival in the 1920s. When I suggested that such a film might not go down too well in Glasgow, Mr Bettany was not interested. He was only concerned with making a good film which was a good commercial prospect.

There is also a lot more to be learned about Alexander McArthur. A major gap in our knowledge is precisely how James Milligan, McArthur's half-brother, fits into the picture. Then Mr Newell told me that he worked with McArthur between 1930 and 1935 in the Glasgow firm of Kirkwood, Mackie & Tulloch.[32] McArthur was supposed to have been a driver with this firm. But according to both Longman's and McArthur himself, he had been unemployed since 1929. Then there are neighbours of the McArthurs who are possibly still alive, and who might know something. Mrs Fullagar mentioned a Highland family called MacDonald at 141 Waddell Street where both the father and son were policemen, and also Owen and Delia McLaughlin, who subsequently moved to Simshill. Then among the papers made available to me by Longman's there is the photocopy of a newspaper article called 'A Ghost Rises From the Gorbals' in 'Kenneth Allsop's Book Column'. Unfortunately, the newspaper is not identified nor is the date given. But it was written around 1957, when the Corgi paperback edition of *No Mean City* first appeared. Allsop says in his article that McArthur's *diary* had been found, and quotes a few sentences from it. Where is that diary now? Allsop also interviewed Charry(?) Channon, the publican of The Stag. He also spoke to Kingsley Long on the phone, who remembered there being the manuscripts of at least 20 novels in McArthur's house. His diary apparently said: 'Got £50 for the old house and all it contains. Minus the manuscripts.' Where are these manuscripts? Did any survive? A neighbour told Allsop that he could remember piles of McArthur's papers in the dustbin after his death. What about the Glasgow lawyer with whom McArthur is supposed to have lodged his manuscripts for his brother? Allsop also mentions a Dutch publisher bringing out a private edition of a book by McArthur called *Born Baker*; I can find no trace of this. And in his correspondence about the plagiarism issue, McArthur states in a letter of 17 August 1946 to the Editor of the *Glasgow Herald* that in 1942, a book of his called *Glasgow Variety* was published by the Glasgow firm of Nicholson & Watson. This contained four long short stories, one of which was 'Born Baker'. According to McArthur, this book was 'banned' after representations by Bilsland. I have been unable to uncover anything about this publication, and as I said above, McArthur's correspondence was becoming increasingly irrational at this period. While

32. Mr Newell, *op. cit.*

41

time has meant a temporary end to my own researches as I write this article, I have a hunch that we may still be able to find answers to some of these questions. I would love to hear from anyone who has any further information about Alexander McArthur and his work.

Finally, a literary evaluation of McArthur's work has still to be made, and there are people far better qualified than I to do this. But this can only be done when all the extant work is available to researchers. Thus I have suggested to both Mr MacLellan and Mrs Wood that they deposit their McArthur manuscripts in the Mitchell Library. They are, after all, an important piece of Glasgow's literary history. I am happy to report that both are actively considering this suggestion.

ALEXANDER MCARTHUR: KNOWN OEUVRES

1. *Published works*:

Novel: (with H. Kingsley Long) *No Mean City* (Longmans, Green, 1935). Paperback edition first published by Corgi in 1957.

Short story: 'Life Renews', in: John Singer ed., *New Short Stories*, 1945-46 (Glasgow: William Maclellan, 1946).

Novel: (with Peter Watts): *No Bad Money* (Corgi, 1969).

2. *Unpublished works*:

(In the hands of Mr William MacLellan):

Novel: *Gus McKellar*

Novel: *The Lodger's Wife*

Novel: *The Blackmailers*

Play: *No Fading Cross*

14 short stories.

(In the hands of Mrs Wood):

Novel: *No Bad Money* (This is McArthur's own original version.)

Six short stories:

— 'Riverside', 10 pp.

— 'Tenement Facade', 13pp.

— 'The Rain Went Off', 20pp.

— 'The Empty Shop', 17pp.

— 'Big Lighty', 30pp.

— 'Social Assets', 10pp.

File of letters from McArthur about the alleged plagiarism of his play.

Play: *The Mystery of Gorbals Terrace.*

TRUE VALOUR: VERA KENMURE'S PIONEERING EFFORTS FOR WOMEN'S MINISTRY IN GLASGOW

ANNE ESCOTT

IT IS six o'clock in the evening of Palm Sunday 1934 in Partick. Over a thousand people throng Stewartville Street, clustering round the Congregational Church and stretching almost down to Dumbarton Road. The church fills up for the evening service but hundreds are still outside when the large doors are pushed closed. At the end of the service mobs reappear, jostling and craning to catch a glimpse of the minister. A car pulls away from the side door followed by a portion of the crowd. But realising the minister is not in the car, the waiting hundreds surge first to one door then to the other. At last, with the crowd weeping and cheering, Vera Kenmure, Scotland's first woman minister, comes out of the front door, enters a waiting car and drives off.

It must have felt like her own Palm Sunday. She had won the hearts of the people but had failed with the institution of the church. After five years hard struggle to maintain her position as pastor, she had preached her last sermon at Partick. Nevertheless, she left that night her hopes high and her faith strong, determined 'still to preach the gospel'.

For a few weeks, she had caught popular imagination in the city as the journalistic spotlight shone on woman-ministry. She served the press well. Just turned 30, a tallish, fashionable woman with bobbed hair, she was 100 per cent feminine in appearance, a contrast to the tweeds and brogues of the feminist stereotype. But the episode hides her gruelling ten year struggle against prejudice. The arena of much of the controversy was Partick Congregational Church. In its handling of the issues cast up by Vera Kenmure's ministry, it perhaps reflected in miniature how Glasgow, at least middle class Glasgow, felt about the ministry of women.

The 1920s was a time of great agitation on the part of women to be ordained to the priesthood. The matter received much airing in the Anglican Church (still unresolved in 1990) and in the Church of Scotland, where organisational sophistication delayed the ordination of its first woman minister till 1969. But the Congregational Church with its flexible structure and liberal possibilities might be expected to have been easy meat. Dr Maude Royden was ordained to the assistant ministry of the City Temple in London as early as 1917 and several women had followed in her wake. But even Dr Royden, prolific writer and speaker, editor of *Common Cause* and able campaigner on behalf of women, met her greatest opposition to equality for women within the church. The Congregational Church gave approval to the ordination of

Vera Kenmure — from *Scottish Congregationalist*
June 1932

women but in practice the very democracy (each church is self-governing and decisions are made by meetings of the whole church — one member, one vote) made the acceptance of women ministers unpredictable and precarious.

The issue of married women's employment was an even greater impediment to Vera Kenmure. The 'domestic ideology' affected the attitudes of women and their work throughout the 19th and early 20th centuries. Vera's mother probably never worked and certainly Census Returns suggest both of her grandmothers were full-time housewives. With the heavy unemployment of the 20s and 30s (in 1934 there were 127,027 people unemployed in Glasgow — some 16 per cent of the working population) married women holding down jobs incurred particularly harsh criticism.

So it was against this background that Vera Kenmure staked her claim to follow her vocation and preach the word of God, first as a single woman, then as a married woman and finally as a woman who also had a family to care for. What personal qualities did she bring to the fight?

Vera Kenmure was born Vera Findlay in the early afternoon of a particularly cold day in February 1904, into the home of her maternal grandparents, 24 Burnbank Gardens, a solid stone built two-storey terrace house in a salubrious area just off Great Western Road in the prosperous West End of Glasgow. She was to spend her childhood, indeed most of her life, within the well-to-do district of Hillhead ('a superior sort of place, the inhabitants being both bein and douce . . . it would seem they were not without a certain snobbery'[1]), leaving only upon retirement and then only to tread the well trodden path to Bearsden.

Both her parents belonged to the new, upwardly mobile middle classes within the city. Her father's family originated in County Down, crossing the Irish Sea in the early 1850s to settle in the new mining area in the town of Galston in the Irvine Valley of Ayrshire, then a bleak, dreary place of single-end squalid miners' houses. It is tempting to see a touch of the novelist Guy McCrone's Arthur Moorhouse in Vera's grandfather John Findlay who, as a young man of 24, left Ayrshire to make his fortune in the city as a tea merchant in the expanding commercialism of the 1870s, gradually working his way to 'douce' Hillhead, and possibly adopting the *Wax Fruit* airs and graces. Certainly he did well enough to have his son John (Vera's father) educated and trained in surveying.

Vera's mother's family had a smoother passage through the 19th century. The youngest of five children, her mother Viola Craig (only 20 at the birth of

1. J. J. Bell, *I remember* (1932).

her only child Vera) lived for most of her childhood in Whitehill Street, an elegant row of tenement flats in the clean, bright and spacious new suburb of Dennistoun. She lived almost next door to the new Whitehill School, of first class reputation, where she no doubt received her education. Her father, coming from a family of Glasgow grocers, had benefited from white collar employment created with the expansion of local government. He was a tax collector for the Police Board, possibly a man of adventurous spirit, certainly well travelled. His wedding in 1870 was celebrated in New York.

Ambition was surely the ground of Vera's family and woven into her upbringing. It was to be expected that Vera, despite her sex, would be afforded every educational advantage. She spent all her schooldays at Hillhead High School manifoldly repaying her parents' efforts by completing her final year in a blaze of glory as Dux in English and Classics and taking sixth place in the Glasgow University Bursary Competition. She went on to Glasgow University, became a prize winner in Latin, Greek and English, and graduated in Arts with second class honours in Classics.

More important than her academic attainments was her openness to the qualities of those of stature with whom she came into contact. One guesses she must have been influenced by her school headmaster Duncan MacGillivray who, some 20 years later, was to contribute an article on 'Enthusiasm' to her first stirringly idealistic Christ Church magazine. 'Enthusiasm is akin to faith: it is faith in action. Those possessed of it have, as in the case of faith "subdued kingdoms, wrought righteousness, obtained promises, stopped the mouths of lions, quenched the violence of fire".'

The major influence of her early life must have been her experience of Trinity Congregational Church, the charge of the Reverend Henry Simpson McClelland, a liberal and adventurous man, whose cultured ministry must have won the heart of the young Vera Findlay. In her own ministry, she followed his ecumenism, extending the hospitality of her pulpit to all denominations; harmony in relationships was the basis of her church government. She always paid tribute to Dr McClelland for encouraging her to go on with her ambition to become a minister when it seemed an impossible goal for a woman. He was an ever present support during the crisis points in her early career.

The course of her pioneering success was less the thrust of ambition or her academic and cultural prowess but more the result of her deep faith in Jesus Christ. Also she was no revolutionist. Outside the church, some of her fiercest critics were women who belonged to the feminist organisations and who felt she was not doing enough to promote their various causes.

The Scottish Congregational College took to their first woman student, 'quietly and naturally, free of anything savouring of "stuntism".'[2] Much later, Vera herself writes of her college life: 'The friendliness and courtesy of my fellow students is a vivid memory. The men must have wondered what a queer specimen to expect in this female student, but they kept their fears to themselves.' Paying tribute to the college principal Dr T. Hywell Hughes, she writes of 'the pleasurable shock I had to find a head of a theological college who did not seem unduly surprised at the idea of a woman divinity student'. But the very compliments admit difficulties: 'It was due to his tactful handling that my interview with the College Committee was so little of an ordeal'.[3] Letters severely critical of woman-ministry came from the pen of the Secretary of the Congregational College. Nor were the acceptance of a woman as a divinity student and the approval of women ministers considered synonymous. Vera Kenmure herself believed she would have to go south of the border for a pastorate.

Partick Church surprised everybody, even themselves, in their call of Vera Kenmure. The origins of the church may have predisposed them to such an act of faith. Partick Congregational Church had been born in 1891 of secession from Emmanuel Congregational Church, Overnewton — a walk-out of some 50 members whose sense of justice and outrage led them to support their minister, Revd James Grant, who was being manipulated to resign and complied to prevent disharmony. However, it had to be said that Partick Church had no intention of considering Vera Findlay for the charge. Their former minister, Revd A. G. R. Sievewright, had preached his farewell sermon in April 1928, whereafter the 15 strong Vacancy Committee proceeded to assess four experienced male preachers.

Vera Findlay was merely on the supply list, filling in one Sunday in August; but she made such a favourable impression that several members and the Vacancy Committee thought she should be asked to preach again, which she did on 9 September. The Vacancy Committee 'by a large majority were of the opinion that she was the most outstanding preacher they had heard and . . . had Miss Findlay been a man instead of a woman they would have had no option but to recommend her for the vacancy.[4] Much debate and several motions and counter-motions ensued, one being to ask two of the men to preach again, effectively forestalling the revolutionary road down which the church was undoubtedly slipping. But eventually three candidates were

2. *Scottish Congregationalist* November 1928.
3. *Scottish Congregationalist* April 1954.
4. Partick Congregational Church *Minute Books*.

proposed and seconded, and the votes were cast 19:55:90 in Vera Findlay's favour.

Thus she received the call into a somewhat dissonant body. The succeeding minutes of the Church Meetings show no more than the usual squabbles. Resignations are announced but no more than one would ordinarily expect. Every pew was filled and extra seating had to be introduced into the gallery for her ordination on 1 November 1928. *The Scottish Congregationalist* is grudging and parental: 'It is a big responsibility she has assumed in taking charge of a city church for her first pastorate, and we hope she will retain health and strength for the work she has undertaken.' Somewhat of a rejoinder appeared in February 1929, ironically reassuring 'many friends in the Union' how well Partick Church is faring, 'particularly in view of the fact that it was supposed to be taking a very grave risk, in being the first Scottish Church to call a woman to be its minister;' and then continues that 'in Miss Findlay they have been fortunate in securing one who bids fair to carry them to greater heights than they have yet attained. In her preaching . . . she has given her hearers great spiritual and moral uplift. . . . Her sermons . . . have gone straight home to her hearers who have shown their appreciation by the tense silence which oft-times prevails. From the very start of her ministry, there have been crowded audiences particularly on Sunday evenings when often the church has been quite unable to accommodate those who have sought admission. Many no doubt came through curiosity, and some perhaps to scoff at a woman preacher but, if so, nothing but appreciation has been expressed and many of her hearers whatever their motive at first have returned again and again to listen.'

Clearly her powers were emerging. Former members attest to her greatness as a preacher. Alasdair Shanks elucidates her more subtle strength when he says, 'It is very difficult to disentangle Vera Kenmure from the effect she had on people. Most of the great divines had some distinctive quality — personal idiosyncrasy — that springs to mind whenever their name is mentioned . . . Vera Kenmure was different. Of course she was an outstanding preacher and she, herself, regarded this as her special gift . . . but there was more to it than that. . . . Consciously or unconsciously, her influence permeated every sphere of the church's activities. This in no way detracts from the quality of the people concerned. It was simply a case of bringing out the best in people — in many cases, qualities they had not hitherto realised they possessed. Yet all this was achieved without any attempt at dominance or dictation.[5]

5. Alasdair Shanks, *Revd Vera Kenmure of Christ Church: A personal reminiscence.* Unpublished. Scottish Congregational Archives, Mitchell Library.

So far, Vera Kenmure had challenged the prejudices of Partick Church alone. By applying for recognition as a minister of the Congregational Union of Scotland early in 1929 she effectively sought the affirmation of every Congregational church in Scotland. Her application was unanimously endorsed at Glasgow District level but received much opposition elsewhere. Dispute raged around marriage, pension rights and Bursary Fund. She was fortunate to have the advocacy of Dr Thomas Templeton who successfully enjoined Assembly delegates to 'Think of principle, and of the spiritual aspect first. Then the expediencies will settle themselves . . . And if a call to the ministry comes to a woman, who are we to bar the way? Haply we might be fighting against God. Our Church boasts its freedom. Let us use it to give a full opportunity of survival of the woman-ministry'. 'And women' was added to the Union Constitution, and all other issues including marriage were left to the individual churches.

And not so very long after, Partick was once more alone on the stage. In January 1933, Vera Findlay put a letter before the Church Meeting intimating her forthcoming marriage to Partick church member and Bible Class leader Colin Kenmure. She offered her resignation, stated her decision to continue in the ministry, and her willingness to remain at Partick should the members so desire it. A Special Church Meeting voted 176:92 that she should stay. But one of her staunchest supporters remarked, upon his resignation the following year, on a gradual change of feelings of many members towards Mrs Kenmure, a process accelerated by her pregnancy. Three weeks after the birth of her son on 31 December 1933, a meeting was called 'to consider the ministry of the church'.

This prompted Vera Kenmure's heart-felt letter of resignation:

'I wish to make it abundantly clear that I do not resign because I find that the duties of a wife and mother are incompatible with those of a minister of a church. On the contrary, I am convinced that my ministry . . . will only be enriched and made more useful by the added experience which these relationships bring. . . . My sole reason for resigning is my strong feeling that the deep opposition and active hostility of a section of the congregation make honest co-operation impossible and prevent me from continuing a successful ministry among them. I will not be the minister of any church where disharmony is rife.'

She remained true to her word and resigned in spite of the slight majority in her favour (159:138).

Within a month of the emotional scenes described at the beginning of this article, Vera Kenmure had realised her hope 'still to preach the Gospel'. In the old Central Halls in Bath Street, on 18 April 1934, Christ Church Congregational was officially constituted and the Revd Vera Kenmure appointed minister. Its core of some 100 to 120 members of Partick Church who resigned along with their minister included a large group of young people who had become accustomed to using Partick Church Hall on Sunday evenings for discussions. One of their number, Alasdair Shanks, takes up the story:

> 'The minister made a point of preaching an evening sermon that would introduce some topic suitable for discussion and eventually most of the congregation simply flocked through to the hall after the evening service. When eventually Mrs Kenmure tendered her resignation . . . the original group of young people got together and decided that they would continue to meet in one another's house and ask Mrs Kenmure to preach/talk to them there. Word of this got round to some of the older members who were also making plans and they advised us that they were planning to hire a hall for the same purpose and invited us to join forces with them.[5]

Christ Church's stirring constitution outlines trenchantly the essence of Congregationalism and continues:

> The five year ministry of the Revd Vera M. M. Kenmure BD has been a blessing to many, and we can find no reason why her ministry should not continue. The reason given by some, that marriage is a barrier to the exercise of her ministry, we cannot accept; for we know of no divine principle which demands a celibate ministry, whether exercised by man or woman.
>
> We have therefore formed this church because we believe that no barrier should be raised against anyone who receives a call to preach the Word of God. We have appointed the Revd Vera M. M. Kenmure as our first minister, not because she is a woman but because we believe in her call to the ministry, and because in matters of the spirit, we do not recognise any disqualifications of sex.'

It is in Christ Church that we clearly see Vera Kenmure's gifts undiluted by dispute and antagonism. She wrote in its first magazine — *The Gateway* — 'I hope the whole atmosphere will be one of friendliness so that even casual worshippers may feel the benediction of it and I trust that many real and deep friendships may be formed among ourselves. And it seems to me that the best recipe for the attaining of such a state is, in the words of ancient scripture "to prefer one another in love" and to be entirely unconcerned about our personal place or dignity'.

The situation at Christ Church demanded even more activities than was normal of church life since there was the constant need to raise extra funds towards a permanent building. The membership worked together and prodigiously, but there was no coercion and no rigid demarcation. Even the traditional division between managers and diaconate (practical and spiritual) was dispensed with. For Vera Kenmure the spiritual world was co-extensive with the real world and vice versa. Nor was there any church roll as such, with the inevitable obsessive task of purging it. The regular membership stabilised at about 270 but infrequent attenders and supporters were always welcomed. Vera Kenmure did not impose upon her members that dampening sense of Christian duty. Duty was not a motivation she liked, and her courage to dispense with it released in her members at Christ Church the eagerness to take part, the joy in working with friends. Within two years, tentative plans for a new church building were well advanced; a site had been provisionally identified; and plans were being discussed which would have introduced some revolutionary ideas in purpose-built church construction.

But just at the high point of a vigorous and exciting venture, Christ Church members were asked for the greatest sacrifice — to let go. Vera Kenmure had received a call to Hillhead Congregational Church. It attests to the quality of the community of Christ Church that they found the maturity to unanimously decide to dissolve the church and enter into fellowship with the members of Hillhead Church. Christ Church was officially disbanded from 27 May 1936, the members rejoicing that the principle of open ministry had been vindicated.

Vera Kenmure spent all her ministry in Glasgow, going to Pollokshields Congregational Church in 1954 from which she retired in November 1967. Thereafter she returned to Trinity, her spiritual mother, and was accepted into membership in November 1968 almost 40 years to the day since her ordination. She died in Aberdeen on 27 December 1973 while visiting her son for Christmas.

Vera Kenmure was not by nature an agitator. Her church was no women's caucus: in fact her congregation had a rather higher then average proportion of men. It is possible that she was relatively unconcerned about the question of married women workers, distinguishing the ministry from a profession or trade as a clear call from God. She must have hoped, as does New York priest Dr Susan Cole King today, to see the ordination of women arrive 'in a way that is gentle enough for people to feel it's not so bad after all'.[6]

Her favourite hymn was 'Who would true valour see', Valiant's song from Bunyan's *Pilgrim's Progress*. She would have had little in common with the militant side of the modern feminist movement; but she would have related to the school of feminist theology concerned to identify feminine spirituality with empowerment. This is in direct contrast to the male view of reality (in the Judaeo-Christian tradition) of powerfulness/powerlessness. She was

6. *Church Times* 15 May 1990.

51

convinced of her peculiar feminine vocation, and her faith never wavered. For its fulfilment, she was prepared to muster all her qualities, talents and energy, for a lifetime if necessary. Like the hymn, she 'caught on' and holds a distinct place in the heart of Glasgow.

NOTE:

I must record my indebtedness to Alasdair Shanks who, as an eye witness, has supplied me with so much information to which, in this short piece, I have not done justice. There is room for a much fuller and deeper treatment of one who must be reckoned among Glasgow's outstanding ministers, male or female.

Thanks also to the present members of Partick Congregational Church for their trust and helpfulness in allowing me access to their church minute books.

THE GLASGOW BOOK TRADE TO 1776

ROY A. GILLESPIE

THE BROTHERS Robert and Andrew Foulis were undoubtedly the outstanding Glasgow printers of the 18th century and have received appropriate recognition by writers on the history of printing. The, perhaps, excessive pre-occupation with the Foulis brother has meant, however, that the work of their contemporaries has been largely neglected. This is unfortunate, not because fine printing has been overlooked — with a few exceptions the Glasgow printers were mediocre enough — but because it has given an unbalanced impression of the Glasgow book trade in the 18th century. Between 1701 and 1800 there were almost 100 printing businesses active in Glasgow and, though the distinction is not always clear, as many booksellers.

These printers and booksellers were more closely in touch with the popular literary tastes of the day than were the Foulis brothers, influenced as they were by the University and the intellectual climate of the Enlightenment. Although one must make due allowance for their superior quality the condition of the surviving books of the Foulis Press gives the impression that they were not much read. They seldom present the dirty and well thumbed appearance of the cheaply produced reprints of sermons and religious dissertations printed in large numbers by the majority of the other Glasgow printers. An examination of the books printed by, for example, John Bryce is far more revealing of the interests of his fellow citizens than is a similar examination of the work of the Foulis brothers.

The merits of the Foulis Press were recognised in their own time and, as a result, there is sufficient contemporary, or near contemporary, material in existence for the compilation of a very fair account of their lives and work. The same is not true of other Glasgow printers and booksellers. They were, for the most part, very ordinary tradesmen and, as such, given no special attention. The first published study of an 18th century Glasgow printer, other than Robert and Andrew Foulis, was Dr Hugh McLean's lecture to the Glasgow Bibliographical Society given in 1913 and published in the following year.[1] In his introductory paragraph Dr McLean said 'with the exception of a few brief notes in books dealing with the history of Glasgow, nothing has been written of [Robert Urie's] life or his practice of the art of typography; this has rendered difficult the work of constructing a biography, as prolonged research has yielded but few details of his life history.' That this could, and still can,

---

1. H. A. McLean, *Robert Urie, printer in Glasgow c. 1711-1771, with a handlist of books printed by or for him* (Glasgow: Glasgow Bibliographical Society, 1914).

THE
PROTESTATION
OF THE GENERALL
ASSEMBLIE OF THE
CHVRCH OF SCOTLAND, AND OF
THE NOBLEMEN, BARONS,
GENTLEMEN, BORROWES, MI-
NISTERS AND COMMONS;

Subſcribers of the Covenant, lately
renewed, made in the high Kirk, and at the
Mercate Croſſe of Glaſgow, *the* 28, *and* 29.
of November 1638.

Printed at *Glaſgow* by *George* ⲥ*Anderſon,*
in the Yeare of Graceↄ, 1638.

be said of the Glasgow printer who ranks next to the Foulis brothers in eminence is some indication of the difficulty of finding information relating to the many Glasgow printers and booksellers much less distinguished than Urie.

Such contemporary material as does exist is far from satisfactory. It is for the most part incomplete and at times ambiguous. Dr Carnie has listed the principal sources for research.[2] They include Burgess Rolls, Burgh Records, Testaments deposited in Record House, the Index to the Service of Heirs, law reports, newspapers and periodicals, the imprints of books and the Registers of Birth, Marriage and Death which, though difficult to use, and often frustrating in their incompleteness and the carelessness with which they were at times kept, contain valuable information. But when one has used all these sources what a paucity of material results, dates of birth and death, dates of printing activity, addresses, the names of wives and children and a few minor events. Poor records of lives which extended for, perhaps, 60 or 70 years.

Printing was introduced into Glasgow, from Edinburgh, in the year 1638 when George Anderson printed *The protestation of the General Assemblie*, but it made little headway. From 1638 until 1713 there was never more than one printer at work within the City.

George Anderson died in 1647, he was succeeded briefly by his wife and children (The Heires of George Anderson) who returned to Edinburgh in 1649.

For eight years Glasgow was without a printer. In 1657 Andrew Anderson, son of George Anderson was persuaded to return to the City where he remained for four years. He was succeeded by Robert Sanders, the son of a Glasgow bookseller and bookbinder. Robert Sanders printed in the City until his death in 1694 when his son Robert Sanders, the younger, also known as Robert Sanders of Auldhouse, took over the business. The elder Sanders had been printer to the University, printer to the Town, and one of His Majestie's printers. His son assumed these appointments.

Robert Sanders, the younger, was neither a good printer nor, to judge from the number of his works which have survived, a particularly active one. The University certainly found him unsatisfactory. Although he continued to print until his death in 1730 he apparently did not print for the University after 1707.

In 1713 the University, having apparently abandoned Sanders, began to look for a new printer. Negotiations were begun with one Thomas Harvie, a

2. R. H. Carnie, 'Scottish printers and booksellers, 1668-1775: a study of source material'. *The Bibliotheck*, 4: 6, pp. 213-27.

student of Divinity, but though discussions and proposals reached an advanced stage no final agreement was made.

In the following year the University made a further attempt to establish a printer of its own. This time the choice was Donald Govan, a merchant in Glasgow, but before an agreement with Govan was reached there was a curious episode involving a printer named Hugh Brown. Brown had begun printing in Glasgow in 1713 and in 1714 issued four works showing in their imprints a connection with the University. One, *The last words of Mr Donald Cargill, when on the scaffold,* was stated to have been printed in the University. The other three described Brown, in one form or another, as printer to the University. The first three printed appear to have brought no comment from the University but the fourth, *The Jacobite curse,* a pamphlet of political intent, brought an immediate denial of Brown as University Printer. He was, it was said, never printer to the University but only employed by Donald Govan who for some months past had been allowed to print within the University. Govan denied all knowledge of the pamphlet. Brown may have been an employee of Donald Govan, probably not himself a practical printer, but he continued to print under his own imprint until 1720.

Govan was officially appointed Printer to the University in 1715 but is not known to have printed after 1718. Although his period of printing activity was a short one he does have the distinction of having been the printer of Glasgow's first newspaper which ran from November 1715 until May 1716, 67 issues in all. Originally *The Glasgow Courant,* the title changed after the first three issues to *The West-Country Intelligence.*

It is perhaps surprising, when one considers the poor success which had thus far attended their efforts, that the University authorities did not turn to two printers who began work in Glasgow shortly before Govan ceased to print. These were James and William Duncan who began printing in partnership in 1718. It may have been that they were too obviously 'commercial printers'. The University predilection seems to have been for the non-professional such as Thomas Harvie, student, Donald Govan, merchant, and later Alexander Carmichael who, though not officially appointed, printed in the University and was the son of a Professor there. Even Robert Foulis, though he had been printing for two years before becoming University Printer could be described as a University protégé since he began his career as a bookseller under University auspices. What they sought, no doubt, was a combination of education and printing ability, a combination which was apparently rare. For whatever reason the Duncans were not appointed but they quickly enough established themselves. Their partnership lasted just two years and they then began to print independently.

William and James Duncan are the first members to be noted of one of the more difficult families in the Glasgow book trade, though the difficulty is one for the genealogist rather than for the bibliographer. The name Duncan occurs again and again in the next 100 years. There are at least three James Duncans, three John Duncans, two William Duncans and a number of Andrews, Alexanders, Roberts and Thomases. Their lives overlap in a most confusing manner and their relationships are almost impossible to establish. It is by no means certain, for example, that William and James were related, though Dr David Murray believed them to be brothers. G. W. Shirley, in his paper on the Dumfries printers[3] suggested that John Duncan, a Dumfries bookseller who came to Glasgow about 1739, was a third brother but though this would establish an intriguing link with the Rae Press at Dumfries the evidence is far from convincing.

Rather more is known of James Duncan than of William. He was a man of parts and in addition to being a printer and a bookseller was a type maker and a paper manufacturer. McUre's *History of Glasgow* which he printed in 1736 is said to have been printed with his own type.[4] It does him little credit. In 1736 he acquired mills on the Kelvin for the manufacture of snuff, oil and paper. His action in building dams, to the detriment of the mills of James Graham, led to assault and battery on the person of Duncan and brought both Graham and Duncan to the Sheriff Court of Dumbarton.[5] The mills were still in the possession of the Duncan family in 1800.

Duncan was a printer of Gaelic religious works for many years but his work was not much to the liking of the Provincial Synod of Argyll. In 1752 Duncan put about proposals for a *Highland New Testament and Psalm Book* which roused the Synod to insert a lengthy advertisement in the *Glasgow Courant* disclaiming all connection with the work and announcing its intention 'without loss of time, to set about an exact edition of the Highland Psalms, which the gross errors of the latter editions, published at Glasgow, renders so necessary.'[6] As the only Gaelic publisher at that time was Duncan the insult was direct. Duncan was undeterred but took note of the criticism, announcing in 1754 that 'he had engaged a hand for correcting it, whose skill in the language had been approved by the best judges.'[7]

3. G. W. Shirley, *Dumfries Printers in the Eighteenth Century* (Dumfries, 1934).

4. John McUre, *History of Glasgow*, 2nd edition (Glasgow, 1830).

5. Court of Session Papers. James Graham v. James Duncan, December 1749 – January 1750.

6. *Glasgow Courant* 30 October/6 November 1752.

7. *Glasgow Courant* 21/28 November 1754.

James Duncan, according to his own statement was born in Glasgow about 1681 and lived there all his life. He died in June 1766 aged 85. William Duncan died three months earlier aged 70.

In 1721 a Thomas Crawford printed an edition of *Napthali, or the wrestlings of the Church of Scotland* and also a number of pamphlets, but for the remainder of the 1720s the only printers in Glasgow were Robert Sanders and James and William Duncan.

In 1730 Alexander Carmichael & Co. printed the second edition of *A believer's mortification of sin by the spirit*, a work by Carmichael's grandfather first published in London in 1677. Alexander Carmichael was the son of Gerschom Carmichael, Professor of Moral Philosophy in Glasgow. He entered the book trade as a bookseller in 1724 when he took over a stock of books acquired by his brother who died before he could set up in business. He may also have been the Alexander Carmichael who was Librarian to the University from 1727 to 1735.

The imprint of *A believer's mortification* gives as place of printing 'Glasgow College' and in the same year, 1730, was published Frances Hutcheson's inaugural address bearing no printer's name but with the imprint 'Typis Academicis' which was clearly from the same press. There were other books with this imprint in following years and it would seem that though Carmichael was never officially appointed he did occasional work for the University. The presses and type probably belonged to the University as there are indications that the same materials were used by Donald Govan, Thomas Crawford (though his imprints make no mention of a university connection), Alexander Carmichael, Alexander Miller and Robert Foulis in some of his early work. Carmichael printed only occasionally for the University; the majority of books bearing his imprint were printed elsewhere, probably on the premises of his partner Alexander Miller in the Saltmarket.

Carmichael's imprints of 1730 are in the simple, dignified form of 'Mr Carmichael and Company' but from 1731 the partnership is set out in full in one of the clumsiest of Glasgow imprints as 'Mr Alexander Carmichael, James Brown, John Brown, Alexander Miller and Mrs Brown in Company.' The Browns gradually disappeared from the imprints and Carmichael's name last appears in 1737 leaving Alexander Miller to print alone. Carmichael died in 1768, aged 72.

In 1738, 100 years after the introduction of printing to Glasgow there were still only three printers in the City, James and William Duncan, and Alexander Miller. Booksellers were rather more numerous but probably only two, Alexander Stalker and John Barry, were solely booksellers. The others, John Robertson, James Brown and Mrs McLean were also, and probably primarily, bookbinders. All three printers on occasion also described themselves as booksellers.

The staple productions of the presses were sermons and religious tracts and even in this field there was considerable conservatism. The works of proven popular authors were reprinted again and again. Among the most popular were the Puritan divines Thomas Brooks and Christopher Love and the Covenanters Samuel Rutherford and Alexander Peden. The sermons of the gifted preacher Andrew Grey were often reprinted and Bunyan's *Pilgrim's Progress* was another favourite.

The 1740s saw great changes in the Glasgow book trade. In that decade eight new presses, some admittedly short-lived, were founded, two newspapers commenced publication, Alexander Wilson and John Baine brought their type foundry from St Andrews to Camlachie, only a mile from the city, and a number of booksellers, including the successful Daniel Baxter began their careers. Of the presses the two most important were undoubtedly those of Robert and Andrew Foulis and Robert Urie.

Robert Foulis was born in Glasgow in 1707, the son of Andrew Faulls, maltman, and Marion Paterson. In 1720 he was apprenticed to a barber and in 1727 established himself in that trade. In 1739 he set up as a bookseller, probably 'within the College' and in 1741 began publishing, with books printed by Robert Urie and Company and possibly Alexander Miller. He began printing on his own account in 1742 and in the following year was appointed Printer to the University. Towards the end of 1746, or early in 1747, he took his younger brother Andrew into partnership and henceforward they carried on the business of booksellers, literary auctioneers and printers under the style of 'Robert and Andrew Foulis'. The firm possessed a binders shop and Robert personally supervised the binding of many of the books printed by the press.

With the exception of the books printed by Robert Urie the books produced by the Foulis Press present a startling contrast with those of its contemporaries. Other than a few of the early works they are completely devoid of ornament, printed with good type on good paper, accurate in composition and register and have title pages of an absolute simplicity. In subject they are chiefly standard classics in Latin, Greek, French, English, Spanish and Italian. Andrew died in 1775 and Robert in 1776. Throughout their printing careers they had fair claim to be among the finest printers in Europe.

The most distinguished printing contemporary of the Foulis brothers in Glasgow was Robert Urie. In octavos and duodecimos he was their match but his few folios and quartos are disappointingly poor.

Robert Urie was born in Cathcart in 1713, the son of Robert Urie of

Holmhead.[8] The family was connected by marriage to a number of landowners and merchants in the Glasgow area. A Robert Urie who took a Greek class at the University in 1728 may have been the printer but unfortunately the entry in the matriculation album is one of the few from which the name and designation of the father have been omitted.

Urie was apprentice to Alexander Miller and began printing in his own right in 1740. He was not alone in the venture, his imprint being 'Robert Urie and Company', but it is not clear who were his partners. There is some evidence from advertisements that they were the booksellers Andrew Stalker and Alexander Carlile, joint publishers of the *Glasgow Journal* which began in 1741 and which was printed by Urie.

During the period in which Urie printed in partnership his work is good without being in any way remarkable, but with the dissolution of the partnership in 1747 there is a marked change. Influenced, no doubt, by the Foulis brothers he rid himself of cluttered title pages, acquired new type, printed on good paper and generally raised the standard of his work. In 1750 he produced what may be considered his finest works, a Greek New Testament and an edition of Buchanan's *Psalms*.

Urie continued as a printer until 1757. In that year the first books bearing the imprint 'Printed for Robert Urie' were issued from what was clearly his press. After that date Urie himself apparently printed only occasionally. It is probable that from 1757 Urie devoted himself to the bookselling side of his business and left the printing to William Smith, another Miller apprentice, who worked with Urie and at his death succeeded him. The arrangement must have been in the nature of a partnership, though not formalised as such, since Urie owned no printing materials at the time of his death. These must have been given or sold to Smith and the printing done for Urie on Urie's premises in the Gallowgate.

Not the least interesting feature of Urie's work is his choice of books for publication. If these reflect his own taste he was a man of some culture with an inclination towards philosophy, history and poetry and with little of his contemporaries' interest in sermons. He printed very few classics in Greek or Latin, perhaps not caring to compete with the Foulis Press, but a large number of translations from the French, in particular the works of Voltaire, Fenelon and Abbé Vertot. In all he printed more than 20 Voltaire translations, many of them within a year of their first appearance in English. He did not, however, indulge his taste at the expense of his pocket as his will indicates a fair financial success. He died in 1771 at the age of 58.

8. R. A. Gillespie, 'The parentage of Robert Urie, printer in Glasgow'. *The Bibliotheck* 5:1, pp. 34-40.

Of the booksellers who began their careers in the 1740s Daniel Baxter was the most outstandingly successful. He was the son of David Baxter, a bookbinder, who died in 1722, less than 18 months after the birth of his son. Daniel was brought up in the Saltmarket by his mother.

In 1743 Baxter married Mary Cameron, widow of Alexander Miller, and entered into business as a bookseller. He was then 22 years of age and Mary Cameron about 42. It may be unkind to suspect Baxter of unworthy motives but the widow's possession of a well stocked bookshop, printing office, bookbinding materials, household goods and a substantial sum of money may have influenced his choice of wife. He was certainly active in her interests and two years later was still pursuing a number of small sums of money due to Alexander Miller.

Although by his marriage Baxter came into the possession of printing presses and associated equipment he did not pursue the trade. He was, however, the partner of Robert Smith and Alexander Hutcheson who printed together from 1743 to 1745. His name does not appear in the imprints of their books but when the press was advertised for sale in 1745 it was described as '. . . the printing press and haill materials for printing thereto belonging . . . that belong to Alexander Hutcheson, Daniel Baxter and Robert Smith, and were in partnership amongst them.'[9]

With John Barry, Andrew Stalker and John Gilmour, Baxter was one of the early encouragers of Robert Urie. He was one of the few members of the book trade to achieve an official position in the City and was Director of the Town's Hospital and a Governor of Wilson's Charity Trust. At his death in 1784 he left half of his estate, about £3,000, to Hutchesons' Hospital, the remainder being divided among a large number of relatives and friends. His wife, though 20 years his senior, survived him by more than two years.

The Glasgow newspapers which commenced publication in the 1740s were the *Glasgow Journal* and the *Glasgow Courant*.

The *Glasgow Journal*, published by Andrew Stalker and Alexander Carlile, was printed by Robert Urie. It began in 1741 and continued for more than a century. Andrew Stalker was the editor.

Stalker first appears in 1726 when he was engaged by Alexander Carmichael to keep his shop for a year. He then spent two years in Edinburgh, returning in 1729 to enter into partnership with Carmichael. The partnership did not last and by 1734 Carmichael was attempting, through an action in the Court of Session, to prevent Stalker from opening his own bookshop on the grounds

9. *Glasgow Courant* 25 August/1 September 1746.

that 'the place was too narrow for two booksellers at a time.'[10] The action failed and Stalker continued as a bookseller until his death in 1770. He resigned his editorship of the *Glasgow Journal* in 1768.

Stalker was probably an Englishman; his heirs, Samuel and John Stalker, were both Londoners and he was one of the trustees of the English Chapel in Glasgow. It may have been for this reason that he temporarily handed over the editorship of the *Glasgow Journal* to Robert Urie during the Jacobite Rebellion of 1745.

The *Glasgow Courant* began its life in 1745 and lasted until 1760 when its editor, Matthew Simson, retired on grounds of ill health and recommended that its readers should transfer their allegiance to the *Glasgow Journal*. The *Glasgow Courant* was printed at the Foulis Press.

Over the next 20 years, 1750 to 1770, the average number of printing offices active in Glasgow at any given time was around eight, though many came and went and partnerships were in a continual state of flux. The principal printers of the period were the Foulis brothers, Robert Urie, James Duncan, William Duncan, William Duncan junior, John Hall, John Bryce, John Robertson and Archibald McLean. Among the principal booksellers were Andrew Stalker, John Barry, Daniel Baxter, John Gilmour and John Orr. Both John Gilmour and John Orr are worthy of note, John Gilmour as publisher and editor of the *Glasgow Weekly Chronicle* and John Orr as the main Gaelic publisher in the city.

John Gilmour began business as a bookseller in Glasgow about 1740 and remained in the trade until his death in 1772. In 1753 he became involved in a quarrel with John Orr and his advertisements in respect of it show him to have been a man of pleasant wit.

The occasion of the quarrel was the proposed publication by Orr of the works of John Flavell, a project which at the same time had been undertaken independently by Gilmour in conjunction with Andrew Stalker and others. Orr in his advertisement had been ill advised enough to criticise the edition proposed by Gilmour and his partners and to this Gilmour replied, also in the form of an advertisement:

> . . . They have found out that another impression is intended by another party, from a design which, it seems, John Orr and Company cannot account for, though without being conjurors, they might have suspected, was the same as their own, a little profit. But it will be still more difficult for the said John Orr and Company to account to the public, how the edition will in many respects be preferable to one that has not yet a being, and of which they have seen no

10. Craigie Session Papers VIII. Carmichael v. Stalker, 1734.

specimen, unless that the said John Orr has brought with him from home the second sight.

Their conclusion, to use their own accurate words, that this edition will be sold at a considerable lower rate. We believe that this is very true, for if in no market it will bring on an equal price with that of the other party, it must be sold lower, or stick on hand; but, to make amends for the low price of their Flavell, we wish the company a high price for their tobacco and checks.[11]

In 1767 Gilmour began publication of the *Glasgow Weekly Chronicle* in competition with the *Glasgow Journal*, the only newspaper in the city since the *Glasgow Courant* ceased publication in 1760. On Gilmour's death in 1772 the paper passed to a fellow bookseller, John Robb, but did not long survive. It is one of the scarcest of Glasgow newspapers.

John Orr, as Gilmour's reference to his second sight suggests, was from the Highlands. He was, presumably, a Gaelic speaker since it was to Orr that the Synod of Argyll entrusted the publication of McFarlane's Gaelic translation of the Psalms saying, in the attack on James Duncan, in 1752, that 'things of this importance ought not to be rashly undertaken, especially by such as have no knowledge of the Highland language.'[12] Orr's edition of the Psalms was published in 1753 and from that date onwards he was the principal, indeed almost the only, publisher of Gaelic books in Glasgow. He died c.1766.

The 1770s saw the end of an era in the Glasgow book trade. Andrew Stalker died in 1770, Robert Urie in 1771, John Gilmour in 1772, Andrew Foulis in 1775 and Robert in 1776. Daniel Baxter lived until 1784 but his name seldom appears in imprint or advertisement in the 15 years or so before his death. With the improvement of communications and the consequent great ease of importing books from London and Edinburgh, the booksellers dominated the scene to a greater and greater extent. Printers' names became less prominent in imprints and advertisements and were replaced by the impersonal names of firms such as Dunlop & Wilson, Brash & Reid, Stewart & Meikle and Morrison & McCallum. The personal character of the Glasgow book trade was much diminished.

11. *Glasgow Journal* 25 June/2 July 1753.
12. *Glasgow Courant* 30 October/6 November 1752.

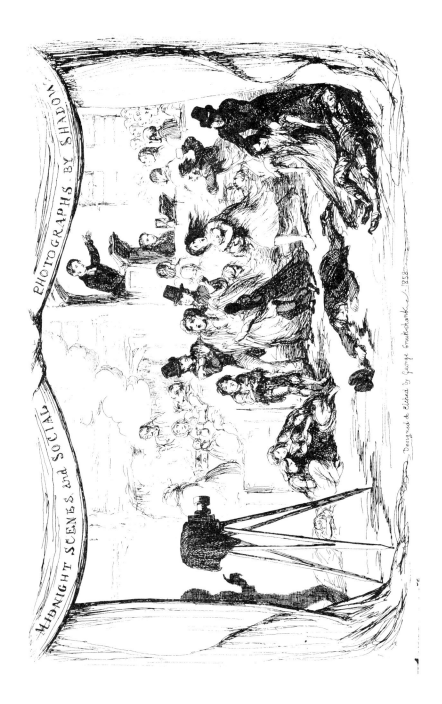

PHOTOGRAPHS BY SHADOW

MIDNIGHT SCENES, and SOCIAL

Designed & Etched by George Cruikshank 1858.

DRINK

WILLIAM HUNTER

There's nothing in being teetotal
And saving a shilling or two.
If your money you spend,
You've nothing to lend,
Well, that's all the better for you.
                    I Belong to Glasgow

ALTHOUGH DICTIONARIES offer about 100 ways to say that too much drink has been taken, for Glasgow that is several ways too few. Local lingo has distilled around 20 extra expressions for drunk. Some have a gusto not always found in dictionaries. Much street wisdom went into stotious, which contains the sound of a body bouncing along a wall. Also full of fellow feeling is blootered. Some words have social history in them: for example, steamboats. It denotes voyagers on Clyde pleasure boats who spend more time between decks than in gazing at scenery. Since their river was a burn, alcohol has been a hobby of the keelies, if not a vocation. Their cup runneth over into their vocabulary.

Preoccupation with whisky, for and against, shaped a part of the city's story. It coloured its reputation. Whatever else the rest of the world thought it knew (slums, violence, Commie agitators, and all that), it had a clear notion of a place awash with booze. Glasgow drank, no secret. Proud choruses of I Belong to Glasgow spread the word. But outsiders had the city's number long before Will Fyffe's song in 1921. More befuddling than the amount of hard stuff Glasgow put away is how other people came to be so uptight about it. How did they know? There has been so much sniffing at the city's breath that it is past time to get personal back. What's it to them? Who (let's not mess about) told them?

Alcohol statistics are a volatile. If only for reasons of sensible laziness, they may be better left alone. Besides, no figures provide 100 per cent proof, or better, than abundantly besotted Glasgow has been much more the worse for drink than other places. Stupendous bevvying was not unknown in Ayrshire mine villages or Aberdeenshire fish ports. Marauding Borderers took an awesome refreshment. Edinburgh judges were more admired for their vermilion countenances than their solemn sentences. Statistical history does not make clear that drinking too much was oftener an old Scottish disease than an English one. What's certain is that accuracy and inebriation are distant cousins. Hardly anybody tells the truth about his own drinking, never mind trying to be exact about other people's. Glasgow's reputation has been exaggerated more than most, although Glasgow asked for it. Getting fu' and then blaming the world for going roon' and roon' leaves no defence.

Being cried steamin' when you weren't, or not especially, can be hard to take. It gets ignored that when the lieges were asked on a March day a long time ago what was their pleasure, they said they would rather do without altogether, thank you. Given the choice of taking drink or leaving it alone, Glasgow in 1887 voted to leave it alone. It chose prohibition. Some of the city's close association with stotiousness, while much deserved, came from its parallel determination, mostly forgotten, to abstain from ardent spirits. Before some heavy bouts of teetotalism during last century, there were simpler days when it was everybody's ambition for at least half of the time to stay at least half-seas over.

Eighteenth-century manners seldom tut-tutted about inebriation. Falling-down behaviour was called conviviality. Even ministers of the Kirk openly enjoyed their brimmers. When they moved to a bigger charge or published a sermon, there were cheers. Alcohol oiled the entire social round. The first week's wages of a tradesman after his apprenticeship went entirely on treating his mates. When servants joined a new house they were paid to have a knees-up with their friends. Since pub licences were seen as sources of municipal income, they were handed out like parking tickets. Every sort of shopkeeper sold drink on the side — barbers, tobacconists, and even bakers.

Gentlemen had their clubs. Every sociable cove who cherished his business connections had plentiful excuses for nights-out. There was a club for every craft and whim. At them the flood of liquid refreshment had been set by the tobacco lords, who were regularly trundled home from the Saracen Head as crumbled heaps in sedan chairs.

One of the curses on the city's drinking story has been candour. Curiosity left few hiding places where a fellow could take his ease unobserved. Even a chap's clubs were not sacrosanct. For there was a nosey-parker chronicler called John Strang. His pleasure was to unearth the semi-secret rites of the gentry in their cups. He had his fun with listing their comical associations. There was the White Wine Club, mainly university types, who went to a rural, riverside tavern in Govan to eat salmon and quaff, not grape juice, but whisky. There was the Gegg Club of young blades who played practical jokes. There was a Dirty Shirt Club, not fond of water. The Rumblegrumpy were a literary lot who met at Ma Anderson's in the Trongate to share whisky toddy and scrambled egg. Rum from a communal quaich was the pleasure of the Grog Cub, where the connection was to be in the sugar trade. A sporting gang, the Groggers, threw quoits and played golf on the Green. According to the excellent Strang, they were early-bedders. They tried to end their sessions before midnight. Not that they didn't enjoy themselves, as John Strang clyped:

> The members, however, or at least the bachelor portion of them, generally continued to suck in as much grog and good humour, at even their shortest sittings, as to return home with a song on their tongue and a sedation on their stomach.

Strang intruded on the home life and dinner parties of the toffs. Their behaviour when in was not all that different from being out with the boys. Tired heads fell in the soup. Bodies disappearing under tables went unremarked. There were limits, though. When a visitor was asked by his hostess whether he preferred tea or coffee and was so far gone as to be unable to choose, then it was taken as his time to leave. By 1815 etiquette changed. When Napoleon was meeting his Waterloo, the mighty topers had reached theirs. Conviviality ceased to be *de rigueur*. John Strang described how it reached its closing hour:

> The fact is that drinking had gradually become less and less fashionable: and the too common occurrence of finding half a dozen at every dinner party borne away home by some of their more potent companions in a state almost approaching to speechlessness and insensitivity, became more and more rare, until the abettors of this over-bibulous fashion entirely disappeared from the scene.

City life was taking a turn. Population had mounted at a lick (about doubling in the 20 years to 1815 to around 145,000). Prosperity grew with textiles, chemicals and iron work. Doing business became more complicated. While there was much money to be made, it became tougher to prosper while half-jaked. Shopkeepers and tradesmen gave up dramming in the morning. More evening entertainment was on offer. Wives expected to be taken to assembly dances and theatre shows. Urban elegance reached the streets. Pavements became popular. There was a new respectability and posh tone. An adornment of fine new buildings included the Queen Street Theatre and the Hunterian Museum. Douceness invaded local government. In 1812 town officials who had been keeping pubs had their moonlighting stopped. Sobersides ruled, John Strang observed:

> An apparent approval of temperance seemed at that time also to have reached even members of the Corporation, who in early days certainly exhibited no great anxiety about limiting their own libations to spring water.

Ordinary keelies, all the time growing in numbers towards their one million, ignored the worthy example of their elders and betters. Public sobriety was not a badge the common herd chose to wear. By the end of the century,

Glaswegian in any language meant drunk. Whisky consumption had become a wonder of the world. Visiting scribes viewed with awe the debauchery and degradation they found. Phrases like 'drink-sodden city' flowed from their pens. Their impressions were accurate enough. They were also easy to write. For the city's whisky trail had been explored for them. Low-life reporting of Glasgow became a fashionable form of journalism after a series of articles in the *North British Daily Mail.*

The city-based *Mail* had a shining zeal for sinking a crusading lance into gutter subjects. It investigated baby farming and sanitation. Hanging about all-night street coffee stalls was a favourite assignment. In 1870 the paper's reporters probed what they called The Dark Side, a sin patch of drinking places and brothels around the Cross. This citadel of sleaze was a tenebrous slum of closes and pends from the Trongate south towards the river to Bridgegate and Goosedubs. Although it spilled into Saltmarket, Gallowgate, and the backlands of High Street, the gaudiest thoroughfares were King Street and Prince's (Parnie) Street. *Mail* reporters reckoned they were into the dirt of 200 brothels and 150 shebeens. Laigh Kirk Close at No. 59 Trongate alone had 20 brothels, three shebeens. The *Mail* reported:

> Drouthy and disreputable characters and thieves turn night into day, prowl till four or five in the morning, every now and then refreshing themselves at the shebeens until they become drunk and disorderly and are carried off to the Police Office, making night hideous with their yells and imprecations.

For running an illegal drum the penalty was £10 or 60 days when the *Mail* met Lizzie, a bright, attractive 17-year-old prostitute who had served the time in prison as a proxy for the owner of the house:

> It was melancholy to see so fine a temple dedicated to such base use. 'Is there nothing that can be done to reclaim this poor girl?' said we to the intelligent [police] officers who accompanied us.
>
> 'Nothing,' was the reply, 'she is lost beyond redemption.'
>
> 'Oh, spare me, spare me this once,' Lizzie cried, 'and I'll never come into this hoose again. I'm just oot frae my sixty days, and, oh, it's real hard to gang back again. Oh, spare me this once.'

Having the *Mail* with them on their night sorties improved the enthusiasm of the police. They received admiring coverage. Their names got into the paper. Their rotten job was made harder by how little right of search they had. In the shebeens they had to catch money changing hands. Earlier in the century, John Strang had been not impressed by the night watch. Low wages attracted feeble and elderly recruits. Cleared from their Highland homes, some of them could not speak English. By the time of the *Mail's* exposure the constabulary remained under-paid, albeit well-led. Officers made the complaints about manpower shortages which they have been making ever since. To lift the denizens of one ill-famed house needed a squad of 80. It meant leaving unwatched nearly all the other property in central district. Policing was chancy. All the bigger establishments had look-outs. Law-breakers dissolved into the walls of the shadowy wynds. For the polis it was hopeless work. Even the city fathers hardly seemed on their side since some of the lowest cribs were housed in town property. Bought to be knocked down in improvement schemes, the ruined buildings were temporarily leased to any takers. A brothel-keeper who rented for £8 a year sub-let for £52. No municipal solution was in sight. Free-wheeling expansion of the city economy was roaring out of control. A new way of urban living was being invented. It was frontier adventure. There were bound to be casualties. Debauchery on the wild side went with the territory.

Worthy, hard-working citizens could readily enough ignore back-street misery, while some of them quite liked a wee taste of naughtiness. Paying customers included burghers whom the *Mail* described as 'highly respectable clients'. Police swoops netted enough beardless youths to suggest ordinary daft night-life. There was a sort of twilight tourist industry. Some establishments served food, advertising ham and eggs, pig's feet, and bowls of broth stiff enough to see revellers through the night. In the gymnasium at Dugie Travers's shebeen on the Trongate there were some swell young boxers to watch. Servant girls on a Sunday night could enjoy meeting for a snack, not knowing that behind the curtain of the pie shop they had chosen was beyond the law. Vigorous wifies insisted on the best of order in their houses. Even the grottiness of everything had its charm, and a prostitute cost a shilling.

An otherwise douce taxpayer could go walkabout for a weekend and be broke but (possibly) not permanently damaged when he awoke with his face on the floor of the cop shop in Albion Street. Damage to the city's good name lasted longer. Fascination with the sin centre endured in the public prints because it was a handy subject. Its compactness meant that fearless chroniclers could get out of it fast. If they had ventured a mile down-river to Anderston, they might have found that sprinkling a few silver coins here and there was less than enough to pay the exit rate demanded by hard doormen. Besides, newspapers always like to rewrite their files. When the Trongate-Saltmarket quarter was razed, scandal-seeking scribes louped the river to Gorbals.

Sustaining such islands of high consumption had been achieved over the drowned bodies of temperance reformers. For whisky city had twin world fame as an oasis of water drinkers. When teetotallers and milder brethren were not fighting each other, they formed a mighty army. Marching across the social map, they sought to change every contour of leisure time. When drained of alcohol, everyday fun and games became more enjoyable, they lectured. Glasgow was said to match Tokyo for its teashops. City Hall concerts rivalled the singing saloons. Sailing down the water offered an abstaining fleet of dry boats. Rechabite parades enlivened the streets. There were temperance novels. A temperance society opened in Maryhill by John Dunlop, a Greenock lawyer, pioneered an international movement. Ironically, Glasgow's pre-eminence had side effects which sustained its reputation for gargling. As city preachers carried the good message about Britain, they referred often to the swamp they were striving to dry out at home. Forests of temperance literature became well-known for their city imprint, great tracts of them being the work of William Collins, publisher and disciple of John Dunlop. They reinforced the idea that there was an obsession with whisky, fiercely for it or against. When anti-drink councillors made themselves a force on the town council, abstemiousness became a heavy player in the municipal power game. The licensed trade took to whimpering that magistrate courts had been converted into temperance lecture rooms.

Before earnest legislation in the middle of last century, pubs had been jolly retreats. Saltmarket had its palaces — flashy saloons, brightly lit, with mirrored walls. Marble fountains played in them. By their watchful care and paternalism, reforming councillors changed these tempting traps into the bare dark-windowed dram boxes of sawdust pubs. (A legend persists that square-toed shoes, a Glasgow invention, were designed to enable perpendicular drinkers to stand closer to the bar.) By banning drink on municipal property, the long arm of Victorian magistrates stretched to keeping hostelries out of council housing schemes until 1961.

Best-laid plans seldom worked as intended. So long as whisky remained cheap it continued to gnaw away at health and happiness. Whatever improvements the crusaders attempted, pagan alcohol somehow bedevilled them. Something was always the matter with efforts to tame the cratur by law. As in the words of Will Fyffe's song, legislation went round and round. Where it came out was not where it was supposed to.

Along with three other overwhelming counts in 1887 against licensed shops, a scarcely credible return from every district gave a household vote of 57,704, against 19,411, for total prohibition. This result of a mountain of a plebiscite took 33 years to start producing the mouse of no pubs in genteel districts like Cathcart and Kelvinside. An earlier attempt (in 1853) at partial prohibition also went agley. Succeeding in closing pubs on Sundays, the new law aimed also to control weekday opening hours. Time was called at 11 p.m. But when the bell tolled for serious drinkers in licensed premises what they did next was crawl to unlicensed ones. Days which ended before midnight were not long enough. Such dimly wakeful hours as were left to inebriated customers were improved in the shebeens which mushroomed in dark places. Some astonishing beverages were consumed. Diluted whisky (five parts of water to one of grain spirit) was given a kick of meths and flavoured with raspberry vinegar or prune juice. Gin was allowed to age for two days. Some of the greedier howff owners worked on a profit of 1200 per cent, and 500 per cent was regular. From a still in a Gorbals tenement one hooch runner carried his supplies in a tin bodice strapped under his coat like a metal semmit.

To explain so desperate a thirst a likely authority is William Logan, a street-wise reformer. For 20 years he was the city missionary, having first seen the light when he had a job with a licensed grocer. He vowed never to touch another drop when he witnessed the amount of secret drinking among housewives. He recalled: 'I soon saw the evil effects of drink amongst tradesmen's wives especially, who not only consumed it on the premises but were anxious to get it entered in their pass-books as sundries.' Because he had prepared for his missionary work on the dark sides of other troubled places — London, Leeds, Rochdale and Bradford — William Logan could take a wide view of the scene. In a book in 1864 he reckoned there were four reasons why Glasgow drank more than its share:

First. It is the wealthiest city in Scotland.

Second. It has the greatest trade, and many traders seem to think they cannot transact their business without drink. The impression is they must treat in order to succeed.

Third. There are more strangers and commercial travellers sojourning within it and men when away from the restraints of home indulge more freely than at other times.

Fourth. There are more sailors in it, and most of poor Jack's money goes on prostitutes and publicans.

Compared with this middle-class sociology, causes closer to the gutter were put into print by another observer who walked the wynds as a hobby. Alexander Brown was a printer with a yearn to write. For a subject he went shebeening. Unlike Mr Logan, he sometimes took a drink. He wrote: 'Suffice it, then, to say that the shebeen keeper gave us a glass of very good ale, though he did charge, we believe, a very good price.' A tumbler in his hand was a part of Alexander Brown's disguise. He called himself the Shadow, seeing himself in the role of an invisible inquirer never noticed by the untouchables. In a day-by-day log of a bold week spent in mean streets he used a colourful pen:

> There, again, are heard the horrid oaths and imprecations of low prostitutes — carrying their loathsome figures about with offensive boldness — flushed with drink, bloated with disease. Others of these sorry unfortunates may be seen haunting the close mouths, spectres of death, rather than objects of life — waiting with restless patience for another victim.

Shadow clocked some whores so ugly they could only work in the dark. His humour extended to pondering what a beautiful city it would be if every pub had a church spire. But his detached style contained compassion. He had the nerve to publish in 1858 the outrageous thought that staying stotious could be the only way for slum people to survive. As he put it: 'How it is possible for the human frame to be supported amid all this, without having recourse to artificial stimulants, we cannot see.'

Philanthropic help and good deeds were abundant. In 1901 the town council started an expensive welfare scheme to reclaim alcoholics by buying for £7500 a beautiful country house, called Girgenti, to be a compulsory clinic. With room for 58 of them, the inmates were decently fed and had medical attention. There was a farm and a walled garden. Punishment was strict. Escaping for an hour meant a day of solitary confinement. But there seems to have been a sensibly flexible way with house rules. Although prostitutes officially were barred, some part-timers (called sly prostitutes in the welfare lingo of the day) were admitted. The guest list was a sadly mixed group of house servants, textile workers, hawkers, a former school teacher. Mary, 24, had syphilis; Agnes, 32, had been a housekeeper who averaged two convictions a week for being drunk and disorderly; Elizabeth, a circus rider and ballet dancer, was the youngest on the books at 17. A part of the cure was a change of environment, explaining the choice of Girgenti 20 miles away in Ayrshire and distant enough, it was hoped, from the bad company often blamed for the women's downfall. Even after three years in the country, however, there is sparse evidence that fresh air did many of them much good.

Organised welfare was always chasing the free-for-all growth of city industry. Only with improved sanitation, less wretched housing, and the hectic increases in whisky prices at the time of the First World War did rescue work begin to look like catching up. Yet even in the depths of the stupor there remained jauntiness of spirit. Glasgow in drink retained a cussed peasant indifference to conventional virtues like having a bank balance to brag about or worrying what the neighbours thought. On a wild Saturday night Alexander Brown etched street pictures which he found funnier than any show at the Princess's or Theatre Royal. With one of his snapshots he might have been doing field research for Will Fyffe's sentimental celebration in song of a Glasgow drunk:

Though oblivious of his whereabouts, like a philosopher he is engaged in apparent contemplation touching the mysteries of the city, while he physically performs sundry undulatory movements in this, to him, merry-go-round sort of world.

While wonderfully round and round goes the city in 'I Belong to Glasgow,' Will Fyffe used to pause between choruses for some gallus working-class patter. 'When you're teetotal,' he explained, 'you've got a rotten feeling that everybody's your boss.' He complained that rich men's money was tainted. 'Tainted!' he cried. 'Tain't yours, tain't mine.' His recitation suggests there is something noble about a drunk in the street because the poor chap is staggering to get home. He is a victim, maybe, of the good folk with the big motors who drink at home when they are not sustaining the town he belongs to as the new Jerusalem of the second city of empire. The worst victims, though, are like those in the record books of Girgenti. In every way, women had the worst of it. Carted to Ayrshire, they blamed husbands who had died or deserted them. Desperately seeking other reasons for their alcoholism, they used words like grief or sorrow. Depression of spirits was another guess. Most of the women in their posh rural sanctuary couldn't read or write. All the time they tried to run away home.

WORKS CONSULTED:

Elspeth King, *Scotland, Sober and Free* (Glasgow Museums and Art Galleries, 1979).
'The Dark Side of Glasgow,' series in the *North British Daily Mail*, December 1870.
'Shadow' (Alexander Brown), *Midnight Scenes and Social Photographs* (Glasgow: Thomas Murray and Son, 1858).
Doings of a Notorious Glasgow Shebeener (held in Glasgow Room, Mitchell Library.)
W. Logan, *The Moral Statistics of Glasgow in 1863 Practically Applied* (Glasgow, 1864).
John Strang, *Glasgow and its Clubs* (Glasgow, 1856).
The Bailie, 19 August 1874.
Handbook on the Municipal Enterprises (Corporation of Glasgow, 1904).
Particulars of Cases in Girgenti Inebriate Reformatory (held in Glasgow Room, Mitchell Library).
Peter Gammond, *The Good Old Days Songbook* (BBC, 1980).

People's Palace, Merchants House
setting with original mortification panels and Luke portrait
loaned from the Mitchell Library
Photograph: People's Palace

BRICKS WITHOUT STRAW — PUTTING A FACE ON EARLY GLASGOW

ELSPETH KING and MICHAEL DONNELLY

The subject matter of the exhibitions staged at the People's Palace in the last 16 years have been researched without exception in the Glasgow Room of the Mitchell Library. Joe Fisher in that time has given unstinting help, advice and encouragement, suggesting unusual source material and providing moral support when the tasks in hand were particularly difficult. Lately, when we tackled subjects such as the strike of the Calton weavers in 1787, so far back in time as to make the likelihood of acquiring new and relevant material virtually impossible, Joe laughingly dubbed us 'the Bricks without Straw Brigade'. In the end, he not only helped us find the straw, but indicated the sources for clay, sand and cement as well.

His retiral from the Glasgow Room will be keenly felt, and we offer this essay on our curatorship as a small tribute to a fellow professional and as thanks to a rare, many-talented, polymathic librarian.

IN THE People's Palace, which is Glasgow's main social history museum, our yet-unfulfilled remit is to tell the story of the city from the earliest times to the present day in an educational and enjoyable way. It has always been our intention to please Glaswegians first, as it is our belief that if the Glasgow people find the display creditable and satisfying, they will not be slow to recommend it to city visitors. Much of the visitor attraction of our collections — regardless of how they are displayed — lies in the fact that the objects are familiar, and are therefore appreciated by the visitors.

Dealing with the early history of the city is a different matter. There are no immediate, obvious or familiar touchstones. We are in uncharted waters, or in a foreign country. In schools the emphasis is on the last 300 years, from the tobacco lords to the present day. The era before the 'civilising' influence of the 1707 Act of Union is not regarded as being of much importance. The magazine *History Today*, a barometer as far as fashion in writing history is concerned, began its special Glasgow issue (May 1990) in 1630, moving swiftly to the last two centuries which always seem to matter most.

It is a pity that the early centuries are so often ignored or discounted, for the events and developments which took place then have as much intrinsic interest and validity. Whilst Glasgow is justly celebrated as a Victorian city, the great industrial city, the Second City of the Empire, and now the phoenix-like post-industrial city, we should never lose sight of the fact that the city is over 800 years old. We hear very little about Glasgow, the bishop's burgh, the 'special daughter of the Holy See', the shrine of St Mungo and pilgrimage centre of the west of Scotland, the university town and seat of learning. The loss of our Catholic material culture through the Scottish Reformation is indisputable, and in addressing the task of interpreting the pre-Reformation centuries in Glasgow, we kept in mind Monseigneur David McRobert's contention that

> It is more difficult to find illustrative material showing the religious ideas and habits prevalent in Scotland 500 years ago, than to illustrate from material evidence the customs of the ancient Egyptians or Babylonians.

The poverty and fragmentary nature of the three-dimensional objects available to us — two bells, some stones, some pottery and the cast of a broken episcopal effigy — reminded us of the last chapter of Umberto Eco's *Name of the Rose* where the story teller returns to the ruins of a once great monastery, burned and destroyed some 50 years before, picks up the tattered and charred fragments of the books (all that remain of a great European library) and tries to record their titles and arrange them in a pattern which makes sense to him.

We began to look upon early Glasgow as a tabula rasa, or as a manuscript which had become so worn as to be illegible, and required to be written anew. Our task was to produce a palimpsest which Glaswegians could understand, recognise, and perhaps decide to re-write if the displays inspired them to disagree and find out more for themselves. We wanted this new Glasgow manuscript to be jewel-like, similar to a book of hours, and pleasing to the senses.

At the same time, we were dealing with problems which are peculiar to Glasgow — the wholesale demolition of Victorian churches of all denominations, and the consequent destruction of Glasgow-made stained glass. The solutions which we obtained accordingly have been effected in a Glasgow context. We decided to use materials from these demolitions as a framework to build upon, drawing a direct comparison between the destruction of the Reformation period 1560-1590, with the even greater destruction of Glasgow's latest demolition period, 1960-1990. The analogies are many. In both instances values were overturned and the material destruction was considerable. There was spiritual anguish, and fragments only were allowed to remain. The new order which followed was and is considered to be a godly triumph.

Building materials and artefacts were used from the following demolitions: Trinity Claremont Church, Pollokshields (demolished 1984, screens and wood); Kinning Park Parish Church (demolished 1987 — organ screen and Victorian floor tiles); St Joseph's R.C. Church, Woodside (demolished 1984 — Gothic brass candlestick); St Kenneth's, Govan (demolished 1979 — stained glass window); Bridgeton Parish Church (demolished 1984 — panelling); St Bride's, Partick (1976 — candelabra); St Andrews-by-the-Green (deconsecrated 1975 — a pew); the Christian Institute, Bothwell Street (demolished 1980 — stained glass portraits of European protestant leaders); Regent Place Church, Dennistoun (burned 1985 — stained glass); St John's R.C. Church, Portugal Street (demolished 1983 — altar screen); the Methodist Church, Whiteinch (stained glass). If we had had the space to spare, the construction could have been some 20 times the existing size of our ground floor east room, full of vistas and with a soaring impressiveness. The available floor space measured 39 x 25 feet. We constructed accordingly and dispensed with the surplus. The display is a strong distillation of some twelve major places of worship in the city which now no longer exist. The fragments which we rescued from them have been rearranged together in an attempt to convey a sense of the distant past as well as the immediate past.

Wood from secular demolition was also pressed into service. A brewery under demolition on the opposite side of the Clyde provided the seasoned wood for the reconstruction of a 17th century Glasgow close of the kind destroyed by the great fires of 1652 and 1677.

This kind of display is very particular to the Glasgow situation. It would not have been possible, comprehensible or even acceptable elsewhere. People from those parts of England where the Reformation left the physical appearance of the mediaeval church almost untouched, or from southern Germany where the churches are still festooned with mediaeval altarpieces, sculpture and painting find the totality of our Calvinist Reformation hard to grasp. Even in Protestant Scandinavia, pre-Reformation church painting and icongraphy were left intact. In Scotland, however, the wipe-out of images and statuary was almost complete. The sole extant pre-reformation image of St Mungo, patron saint of Glasgow, survives in Cologne Cathedral in Germany; the last remaining image of him in Glasgow was hunted out and destroyed in 1642.

PAINTING THE PAST

The lack of any pre-18th-century images of Glasgow afforded the opportunity of some new commissions. The artist chosen was Virginia Colley, a recent graduate of the Glasgow School of Art, whose work and technique shows a sympathy with and understanding of the medieval period. She painted a view of Glasgow, accompanied by a Breughelesque interpretation of the trades of the time, and a description of Glasgow from John Leslie's *History of Scotland* (1570). The lavishness of the praise of the latter is reminiscent of some of the prose in the 1984 'Glasgow Miles Better' campaign, a link with the past with which Glaswegians of this generation can identify.

The story of St Mungo required some special treatment and an unorthodox solution was found in the massive but defunct hulk of the Glasgow Stock Exchange clock, designed by J. J. Burnet as part of the fabric of the Stock Exchange building in Buchanan Street and made redundant in 1966. In a small museum where space is at a premium, and where 1000 years of history has to be poured into a tiny area, each object in the collection must earn its keep. The gothic form of the clock suggested itself as an altarpiece, and the artist used it like a canvas and overpainted it with interpretations of the St Mungo legends. It is now a teaching piece on the legends as well as an object of beauty. Similarly, she recreated one of the 'papist boards' mentioned in the Glasgow Kirk session records in the period 1574-1642, using panelling from a demolition site and painting it with the image of 'Beate Maria in Sole', (the Woman in the sun of Revelations XII) from the Arbuthnott Hours in Paisley Museum. An identical board was painted white and inscribed with one of the Gude and Godlie ballads which emphasises the revolution against 'graven images' and 'monuments of idolatry':

Quha dois adorne Idolatrie
Is contrair the haly writ
For stock and stane is Mammontrie
Quhilk men may carve or quhite
The Apostillis that wraite the veritie
Expresly do conclude
That Idoles suld detestit be
As contrair to Christis blude.

BISHOP WISHART AND THE WAR OF INDEPENDENCE

The central feature of the medieval section of the display is the recumbent effigy of Robert Wishart, Bishop of Glasgow 1273-1316, who supported first Wallace and then Robert Bruce in the long struggle for independence against England. The original was all but destroyed, probably at the time of the Reformation, and survives without head, hands, crozier and supporting angels in the lower church of the Cathedral. In the early 19th century parts of the tomb chest, including a high relief carving of Wishart, were removed to Paisley Abbey to repair the contemporary tomb chest of Margery Bruce. At about the same time the contents of Wishart's tomb were destroyed by a young vandal called Archibald McLellan who in later life 'restored' the Cathedral by demolishing the two medieval western towers (1847) and gifted a gallery and fine art collection to the city.

With the original effigy available for inspection less than a mile away in the Cathedral, we felt justified in attempting to reconstruct and paint the plaster cast of it in the collection to give an impression of how it might have looked when it was first made. A sculptor from the School of Art restored the figure, replacing the missing angels at the bishop's head and the praying bedesmen at his feet. The toes of the latter can be seen clearly on the original effigy, making it significantly different from the dogs or lions who usually support the feet of ecclesiastics of this period. We also took the opportunity of casting the tomb chest in Paisley Abbey, so that the constituent parts of the figure could be brought together, probably for the first time in over 400 years. Advice on the colour for this and other historic stonework was provided by Charles Burnett, Ross Herald.

In many respects Robert Wishart is the forgotten hero of the War of Independence. We used modern representations of Wallace (a white marble Victorian bust) and Bruce (a maquette based on the Great Seal of Scotland, by C. de O. Pilkington-Jackson) to tell the story. In this section we also included the magnificent pulpit seat from Dowanhill Parish Church, decorated in a distinctive neo-Gothic style by Daniel Cottier (1838-1891) and gifted to the museum by the Minister and Congregation in 1984. The pulpit seat decoration was found intact under the later coat of emulsion, whilst the missing crewel work from the back of the seat was reconstructed from the evidence of an old lantern slide by a member of the Embroiders' Guild.

For 1990 only, we were able to obtain on loan the Stone of Destiny or Lia Fail, taken by Edward I in 1296, repossessed by a group of Scottish nationalists in 1950, copied by Glasgow stonemason Robert Gray, and given by him to the Minister and Congregation of St Columba's Parish Church in Dundee.

PUTTING IN THE POETRY AND PEOPLE

At different points in the display, we attempted to include some of the language and poetry of the time. Beside the cast of the portrait of Alexander III from a boss in the lower church of the Cathedral is the poem 'When Alexander our king was deid'. Above the Wishart effigy is inscribed his stirring rebuke to Edward I, put into his mouth retrospectively in rhyming Scots by the chronicler Wyntoun. Dunbar's poetry is used in the section on death and plague, while other rhymes and sayings are used as graffiti on walls.

The character 'Labour' from the 1549 'Complaint of Scotland' was personified as a figure, by way of explaining the politics of the time. In his hands he holds his complaint to his mother, Lady Scotland, in its original Scots with a translation in English on the wall behind.

Marget Holm, who appears in the Glasgow Kirk Session Records of 1602 charged with 'huirdom and harlotrie' is likewise personified, her mouth clamped with the branks. The figures were modelled on contemporary Glaswegians where appropriate. Fish shop worker Betty McAllister for example served as the model for the fish wife in the 17th century close setting.

Different methods of labelling were tried at different points to sustain visitors' attention. Information on the Cathedral and its altars is, for example, presented in the form of a chained book.

STONEWORK AND THE REFORMATION

As we could not contemplate major construction work to build historic stonework in an architectural context, many of the stones in our collection were cast, to enable them to be used in this way. There are no advantages to be gained in displaying stones sitting on the floor, and unless their original purpose is indicated, the public can be confused. The Govan hog-backed stone is displayed with some human bones protruding beneath, to indicate its purpose immediately as a tombstone.

A remaining window lintel from the Eddleston Manse, carved with the inscription 'Domus Edilston' and a Compostella cockelshell or pilgrim's symbol was cast twice to produce windows in a before and after tableau, pointing up the destruction and reconstruction of the Reformation period. A window from Regent Place Church, Dennistoun, designed by William Dyce and rescued after vandalism, fitted the aperture and the purpose neatly in its smashed condition. In the 'after' window were fitted the portraits of the protestant Reformers (Knox, Buchanan, Huss, Luther, Calvin and Zwingle) rescued from the demolition of the Glasgow Christian Institute. Pages of pre-Reformation missals and song books, found in the later bindings of Glasgow Council and Trades House minute books in the City Archives, were colour photocopied and torn up to emphasise the destruction of manuscript material, along with part of the wrecked altar screen from St John's, Portugal Street, inscribed 'Dulcis Virgo Maria' (sweet virgin Mary — the last words of the hymn 'Ave Maris Stella').

The Eddleston Manse stood on the north side of Rottenrow and we know nothing of its physical appearance. For the purposes of its representation in the museum display, the wall panelling came from Bridgeton Parish Church and the wood for the ceiling from the demolition of the Hutchestown brewery which also provided the materials for a partial reconstruction of a 17th century tenement with timber overhang. A rather plain 18th century pew from St Andrews-by-the-Green served as a seat for the figure of Andrew Melville (1545-1622) who is known to have lived in the house at the invitation of its post-Reformation occupants, the Hays, who brought him to Glasgow to reform the University in 1574.

The hoard of pre-Reformation gold discovered during the demolition of the Eddleston Manse in 1795 and reported in the *Glasgow Mercury* of 13 January, suggests something of a panic before the Hays took possession. A copy of the report is included on the information panel, and the hoard is reconstructed under the trap door in the floor, to provide visual reinforcement for the visitor.

THE STOCKWELL MANSION

While the aforementioned displays were conjectural constructions, the Stockwell Mansion display consists of original 17th century material, rescued from the demolition of 1976.

The Stockwell Mansion had a chequered history. Stone built for George Johnston, Dean of Guild, it was requisitioned by some of the Jacobite generals in 1745. It later became the Garrick Temperance Tavern. Jenny Lind sang there. The Anti-Slavery Society held its meetings there. The first Glasgow Trades Council was established there. It ended life ignominiously as the Stockwell Bargain Centre and Bonny Bingo.

When demolition was first proposed in 1976, we examined the house. It had lain disused for a number of decades, and the last serious examination had been undertaken by our predecessor Thomas Lugton in 1905. He confirmed that the original 17th century panelling was intact, and on the overmantle in one of the principal first floor rooms he discovered traces of a painted scene. The panelling had not changed much, but we were totally unprepared for the colour scheme which we uncovered under the centuries of paint layers. Bright red and blue panelling with yellow marbled cornicing had been painted to produce a stunning effect, probably by a Scot who had heard about Italian marbling from travellers' tales. We took the main elements from this room, stripped them, and put them together again, reducing the material to fit the display area.

Only one comparable interior in Scotland survives. It is in Milne's Court, High Street, Edinburgh, and was restored by Rab Snowden of the Stenhouse Conservation Unit in the 1960s. The colours are more muted, but the ice-cream-parlour effect is similar. This kind of scheme is not what comes immediately to mind when thinking of 17th century Scotland and its survival is a helpful corrective to those who are tempted to envisage the period in terms of gloomy Calvinism. For this reason alone we felt the panelling to be worthy of rescue and restoration.

The Stockwell Mansion was the last 17th century building to survive in Glasgow. Although the ground floor has been greatly altered, the rooms in two upper floors survived with their 17th century panelling either intact, or with 18th century additions. The latter, when stripped away, revealed the earlier schemes beneath. The original roof timbers were intact, each marked with a Roman numeral, and the pegged sarking which held the slates in place was still there. However, access from the ground to the upper stories was by a rickety ladder, and because the windows had been bricked up and the premises left full of sulphurous packing cases, none of the agencies responsible for the recording of historic buildings wished to risk limb and camera equipment to record it.

In the end, a record was made by Scottish Television. David Martin of the Planning Department, conservator Ken Gibb and a few friends worked in their own time to help strip out the panelling, for the building, dismissed as an 'insignificant fragment', had to be demolished for demolition access to St Enoch's Station.

The stripping-out process revealed many interesting features, as well as the debris of the centuries — a forgotten tin mug, pottery and glass fragments, and even a full bottle of Glenlivet whisky planted beneath the floorboards when the house was a Temperance Hotel. (Tramping the demon drink underfoot was one of many symbolic punishments of whisky.) The pilaster bases in the room which we have partially reconstructed in the display were packed solid with grain, no doubt as some kind of good luck wish for the house. Some of these items are included in the museum reconstruction.

Some of the panelling was used as a basis for a reconstruction of part of the 1650 Merchants House. On it we were able to hang the original mortification boards, complemented by four of the Luke family portraits loaned from the Mitchell Library's Stirling bequest.

Demolition of the Stockwell Mansion was hastened by a mysterious fire in the adjoining tenement, and we were lucky to save what we did. Although criticised by others for wasting valuable storage space on what looked like junk we feel that the exercise was worthwhile. We have tried to clothe the display using available information. While we knew nothing of the physical appearance of George Johnston, we knew that he would more than likely have worn a blonde or light coloured wig. Gabriel Neil, the antiquarian, salvaged documents from the huge bonfire of records during the demolition of the Cathedral towers in 1848 which showed that Glasgow merchants ordered their wigs from Scandinavia. He believed that

it has been in the reserve of this generation alone, through the salvation of this Document from the fire, to know the *important fact* of the true colour of the hair of those wigs, which were made from the flaxen ringlets of the Swedish and Norwegian damsels . . .

So much of Glasgow's material culture has been lost through demolition, fire and wanton destruction on a massive scale. It is probable that the fragments which we rescued, and which were available to us already in the museum collection, would prove more of a puzzle than a solution to our ancestors, should they have been able to view them. However, we hope that the visual language which ties the display together is a recognisable one, and that it is a creditable basis from which the visitor can obtain a sense of our distant past. If it proves to be a visual document which provokes thought, debate, and disagreement, or acts as an inspiration for people to look again at the history and literature of the period, it will be working well.

QUEEN'S PARK F.C.'s NEW HOME.

The Opening Ceremony.

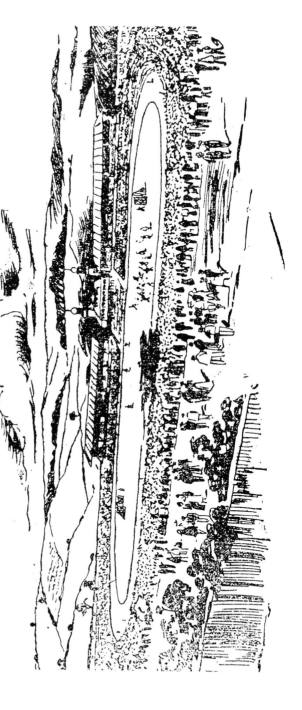

'THE COMMON JOY OF THE PEOPLE'

KEVIN McCARRA

FOR THEIR centenary match the Scottish Football League took us back to the beginning of the century. Hampden Park has been crumbling for decades but the dereliction was particularly apparent that balmy August day in 1990. The game crept painfully along and even the pitch looked exhausted. Near one corner flag there was an ugly slash 20 yards long. This, presumably, was the result of the summer's major rock concert. The Rolling Stones may gather no moss but they can certainly knock hell out of your turf. Although the national stadium has not remained entirely undeveloped, its original, 1903 outline is easy to see. The air of dilapidation is unmistakeable. A little longer and architecture will turn into archaeological remains.

The present Hampden certainly provides a direct route to footballing antiquity. The design managed to slip a few keepsakes of the sport's past into its back pocket. At the beginning (the late 1860s) crowds were kept back from the pitch by ropes and, indeed, their flimsiness allowed more than one fan to lunge forward at the opposition's flying winger. Since there was no banking at first, that cord was arranged in a wide curving sweep around the pitch, thus creating a vast perimeter so that as many as possible could stand at the front and enjoy an unobstructed view. Hampden preserves that notion in its oval shape. Celtic Park has been called 'the best 19th century ground in Britain' but that booby-trapped compliment could also be directed at Hampden.

Lord Justice Taylor's findings and FIFA's insistence on seating render the national stadium obsolete but, at the time of its opening in 1903, it was an attempt at constructing the future. Then, the *Scottish Referee* claimed that Hampden was intended to be proof against 'the ravages of time's effacing hand'. Yet, the builders' hopes deserve better than our sardonic laugh. On 5 April 1902, 26 people had fallen to their deaths at Ibrox because the terracing there was a rickety, wooden construction. At Hampden the banking rested on solid, earthen mounds. New Hampden (it was the third ground Queen's Park had built) also attempted to counter the risks caused by surges in the crowd. Originally, steel cable was used to create discrete sections, each holding 80 spectators. It was not until 1928 that these were superseded by the rigid crush barriers more familiar to us.

The ground was a novelty. Fascinated newspaper accounts dwelt lovingly on the installation of Ellison's patent turnstiles. They clicked in earnest on 31 October 1903 for the first match at the venue, a League fixture between Queen's Park and Celtic. Beforehand, the Lord Provost, Sir John Ure Primrose,

85

Bart unburdened himself of a tedious speech and unfurled a new flag. After 'the manly rivalry was fought out to a finish' the inaugural victory was chalked up to the home side. The only goal was scored by winger David Wilson, who died during the First World War.

The 38,400 who headed for Mount Florida that day were also indicating the direction the sport was taking. They brought with them £800 of gate money. Such toothsome income was hard to ignore. Previously, Queen's Park had vied with Rangers and Celtic to host the increasingly lucrative international games. At the time Hampden was opened, a cartoon appeared showing a thoughtful postman wondering where to deliver a letter addressed 'The International Venue'. It surely contained a large cheque. Building the ground was a gamble, for Queen's Park had only £5000 in hand, half the sum required for the purchase of the land alone, when the club's committee embarked on the project in April 1900. Yet, it was to pay off handsomely and, until recently, the ground's right to host the tribulations and triumphs of the Scotland team, in addition to Cup Finals, has hardly been questioned.

Hampden Park demanded respect from the outset. The journalists of 1903 had to labour strenuously even to produce a tiddler of a quibble. The *Scottish Referee* complained in esoteric manner that, because of the corrugations in the iron, a painted 'public entrance' sign could be misread at a distance as 'no entrance'. This does not seem to have prevented many from gaining access. Hampden prospered steadily in the succeeding decades. In 1914, for example, the present four-storey pavilion was built at a cost of £4700 and in 1927 the terracing was expanded to create room for 25,000 more spectators. With the opening of the precipitous North Stand in 1937 the capacity increased to 150,000.

The stadium's most vibrant days had arrived. On successive Saturdays, the international with England and the Scottish Cup Final brought a total of almost 300,000 people to Hampden. The 149,415 who came for the first occasion still constitute the record attendance for a football match in Europe. Dealing with them brought on skittishness in officialdom. When the SFA worries over matters of millinery the game is in a state of ferment. Bowlers were out of the question. For one day at least, they suggested, bunnets were the gentlemanly response to inclement weather. The administrators were concerned less with the sartorial and more with sight lines. What hope for wee men stuck behind people with overbearing hats?

Two years previously, fans had been left to pay at the turnstiles and, amidst chaotic scenes, 30,000 had been locked out. In 1937 the organisers quivered with zeal as they set themselves against any repetition of that fiasco. It was as if martial law had been declared. Three separate routes to the ground were designated and marked with colour-coded posts. Anyone attempting to pilot a car on a path of their own devising was liable to be fined. The vehicle regulations were uniformly draconian. No-one could even approach the Mount Florida area without showing a pre-paid parking voucher. Radio cars toured the streets reporting all to central traffic control.

The mood of innovation spilled over even onto the pitch. The new goalnets were coloured green, not as a means of brightening subdued Hampden but because they had been coated with a special paint which promised longevity. They were to take in a haul of four goals, three of them going past the English keeper. Scotland preened itself over a victory and an event so successfully managed. Reality did demand some concessions, however. There were those who had to be parted from the notion that the national amphitheatre ought to be capable of accommodating the entire population. Up to that point, the SFA had believed the terracing alone to be capable of holding 180,000 but the vagaries of an actual match dispelled such ideas forever. Many thousands at the international only sighted the ball on the sporadic occasions it was skelped skywards.

At the time, the press insisted that increased efficiency could solve such problems. Spectators, they concluded, must not be allowed to congregate at the top of the terracing, leaving pockets of inaccessible space lower down. In those days of brawny optimism, one suggestion called for 'improved means of passage, by tunnel if necessary'. The idea of a honeycombed Hampden was never to be realised. A pity really; it is pleasing to daydream of a tammied troglodyte bursting a trapdoor in the pitch to thwart some foreigner with mischief in mind.

In the 1930s Hampden was a place where the imagination could play. A 1937 cartoon depicts it in ten years' time and portrays footballers in space cadet garb, a plane landing beside a modernist stand at the touchline and a robot referee. There have been periods in the present day when the transistorised official has seemed a likelier prospect than a re-built national stadium. With that victory over England the expansion of Hampden came to a close. It had been a typical product of the age. The same tolerance of new ideas which allowed commercial builders to sell strikingly original housing in areas like Newton Mearns and Bearsden also gave rise to the dynamic schemes for Hampden. Behind the confidence lay money, and behind it lay the forces which would eradicate the brief prosperity. The revival was stimulated by the need to arm for the imminent conflict of the Second World War which would then leave among its casualties a crippled economy.

In one sense or another, Hampden was finished. It existed thereafter as a place for gathering myths, memories and anecdotes. So, for example, the habit has grown up of locating the creation of the 'Hampden Roar' in the moment in the England game of 1933 when McPhail set up McGrory for the winner. The combination of a Rangers and Celtic player, shelving their workaday rivalry, was viewed as the last word in patriotism. It is of course preposterous to try and set out a lineage for something so commonplace (and magical) as the cheer of a huge audience but, none the less, to say so gives rise to the *frisson* of sacrilege.

The memory of such occasions produced a certain impishness in Bob McPhail. He was still in the Scotland side and scored twice on the day that record attendance was set in 1937. Many years later he became involved in a casual conversation with a stranger who had no idea who McPhail was. This gentleman complained of the terrible crush that afternoon and was utterly mystified when McPhail replied, 'There was plenty of room where I was.'

The attraction to Hampden is not simply a matter of numbers and noise. After a single scene has received so many decades of scrutiny, small details become an essential part of its character. The goals themselves survived, apparently, from after the Cup Final riot of 1909 until they were replaced in 1987 by the meanly-designed variety which are now standard issue. The set which lasted all those decades comprised square-sectioned posts and crossbars. These were distinctive for most of their life and provoked joyfully inconclusive debate. There have been celebrated shots which have rebounded clear from the underside of the bar and left heartbroken supporters with a grievance. They are apt to insist that the ball would have crossed the line had it only struck one of the more usual, rounded crossbars. At least the stanchions tended simply to provoke appreciation. The net strained to cover their generous arch and the amplitude suited Hampden's great bowl.

Even at its freshest, though, the place left you not with an impression of grandeur but of gravity. As the *Guardian*'s peerless football correspondent, David Lacey, once wrote, 'It must be the only ground in the world which, apart from the grass, looks much the same in colour as in black and white.' His exemption of the turf from the monochrome vista only goes to show that he can never have visited Glasgow on a real winter's day.

Until comparatively recently the very fabric of Hampden was spartan. Glamour was not on offer. Everywhere you looked there were reminders that football is essentially a humble game. Until a programme of concreting was completed in 1983, the terracing was composed of ash held in place by wooden risers. Once you had ceased musing on the doubtful safety of the venue the appearance could be curiously resonant. A little way down Cathcart Road the Queen's Park recs, scene of so many schoolboy matches, were then covered in the same blue-black ash as was to be found beneath your feet on the terracing. Between exalted Hampden and those mundane playing fields there was, quite literally, common ground.

Football is composed of large expanses of fallibility flecked very, very lightly indeed with perfection. No regular attender at Hampden Park is liable to forget the fact. It is one of the charms of the ground that it encompasses not only the highest levels of accomplishment but also the whole-hearted clumsiness of the Second Division in which Queen's Park now play. I was allowed, in my youth, to go only to Hampden because my parents judged that there was no risk of the 'trouble' that might be encountered in other Glasgow grounds. Despite periods of remission (I can recall an old man in tears of happiness when Queen's Park scored five against Brechin at New Year 1972) there wasn't much risk of excitement either.

I learned in consequence that football's ability to beguile rests on far more than the passions aroused by the great and well-attended matches. In general, going to a game is an experience about as hedonistic as taking the dog for a walk. At those lowly League fixtures at Hampden there was every opportunity to study the look of the place. There were too few spectators to seriously obscure your view of the naked architecture. Ever since, I have instinctively associated football with tranquility rather than bedlam.

Now, Hampden must either be transformed or abandoned. Plans for its reconstruction have lain dormant for too long. In 1980 a development programme was about to begin but the Government withdrew its backing after Rangers, then beginning to build the impressive modern Ibrox, indicated that they thought such expenditure unnecessary. Some work has taken place since but, essentially, the only thing to have progressed has been the estimated costs. Refurbishment schemes once put at £11 million would now require £40 million to be implemented. The present strategy stalled when the Secretary of State for Scotland refused planning permission for a shopping centre on the lucrative site of lesser Hampden. An appeal is currently under way.

It is virtually certain, however, that FIFA's requirement of all-seater stadiums will ensure that Scotland's next set of World Cup fixtures, beginning in 1992, take place at Ibrox. With the consortiums behind 'super stadiums' in Lanarkshire or Renfrewshire still vague about how they might raise the £150 million or so required, Rangers' owner David Murray believes that his ground should become the new home for the national team. If football were simply a matter of fixtures and fittings this would constitute a happy solution. Ibrox, which continues to expand, has a plausible claim to being the finest football ground in Britain. Stadiums, though, are symbols as much as buildings and in a country as divided as Scotland Ibrox could never command enough support to lift it free of the old tribal associations. It would lack widespread acceptance as the focal point of the dreams and hopes of a nation. For the same reasons, any putative New Celtic Park would be ruled out.

Hampden Park has always been convincingly neutral territory. Mount Florida, if not quite middle class, is remote from the East End of Glasgow, with its history of heavy industry, and from the shipyards at Govan. When the first Hampden was closed down, it was replaced by a bowling club. Where else in Glasgow would football be succeeded by a sport ambulatory in nature but sedentary in spirit? The impression of Hampden as a retreat was even stronger in 1903. The *Scottish Weekly Record*, a journal given to recounting the doings of detectives and reporting on 'Crimes of the Week', assumed a wistful tone when it reviewed the new stadium. It conjured up sylvan delights: 'the open panorama of woodland and hill country to the south should charm the eye of the visitor'.

If the national stadium must be the property of one club, then Queen's Park are the ideal choice. In Scotland, only an anomaly will do as a host. When professionalism was legalised in 1893 Queen's Park clung to their amateur status and have retained it ever since. A decision which was to end their days of winning trophies also gave them a critical edge when the battle to stage international matches was at its height early this century. They stand remote from the fray and that powerlessness gives potency to their credentials as the game's custodians.

A rebuilt Hampden Park remains Scottish football's best hope. After the first match in 1903 the *Scottish Referee* recorded: 'The joy of the Queen's Park players, officials and everyone connected with the club was the common joy of the people'. It should become so once again.

SUFFER THE LITTLE CHILDREN

CARL MacDOUGALL

I USED to have a weekly newspaper column; a regular acquaintance with which makes some members of the public more than usually ready to write to me. I suspect there is something about reading the paper which makes the writer less of a stranger than if he were, say, the author of a book.

It also means the *Evening Times* can suggest pieces for me to do. This had never happened until Ron Clark, who works in the Features Department, suggested to Bob Jeffrey, the chief assistant editor, that I might be able to construct a piece from a reader's letter. It came with two snatches which appeared in a column written by Jack House.

The letter is undated. It was written by Mrs M. Docherty who lives in Longstone Road, Cranhill, who had seen some television programmes about adoption and fostering.

'A problem has had me worried all my married life, that's over 50 years now,' she wrote. 'Over these years my husband now and then tells me harrowing tales about his own childhood experience. Can it be that Glasgow Corporation then, about 70 years ago, had no care or thought what happened to young people. I have many a time wondered at this. There he was, a wee boy aged seven, because of differences between his parents, he was living then with his Granny, and suddenly without any warning he was escorted to the Central Station and there he was met by an elderly man, taken on the train, then onto a boat where he reached the Isle of Barra. From then he tells me his life was one long nightmare, the school he was sent to only taught in the Gaelic, he was tormented, teased unmercifully, then after school hours he was made to work on the land. He never once was allowed to stay in their house, an outhouse with straw for a bed was his home for many, many years. Not one word of kindness was ever given to him. I expect there must be other cases just like his. I know that this will never happen now to children and what a good thing that is. I would be interested to know if these people in Barra did get any payments for fostering, if they did, he certainly never knew.'

The first cutting is from 24 February 1990. Mr W. R. Laird of Mennock Road, Cathcart, writes to Jack House: 'I have received a letter from my uncle in Omaha, Nebraska, who left Dovehill School, near Glasgow Cross, when he was 12.

He wants to find out about the scheme which was available through a Glasgow doctor who arranged for young boys to be taught farming and were

91

then sent to Canada, via Halifax.

Could it be Dr Barnardo?'

Jack House's reply says, 'This question is answered by Jack Dunnett of Gilmerton Street, Sandyhills, whose letter arrived at the same time as Mr Laird's.

He writes: "Have you any gen on Dr Cossar who ran a Boys' Club in Saracen's Head Lane and who could arrange for any of us boys to emigrate to Australia, New Zealand or Canada to be contracted to farmers?

He would kit us out with a new suit, underwear, bonnet and half a crown. It would be nice to hear from any surviving boys."

The second cutting, dated 10 March, recalls 'the famous Dr Cossar of Uddingston, who had a scheme to send deprived boys to Canada to work on farms there.'

P. Wilson, Balgonie Road, Mosspark, writes: 'I was one of Dr Cossar's boys. I started going to his gym in Saracen's Head Lane where we had tea and buns, then sang one or two hymns.

When I took his offer of arranging my training for farming, he gave me a thorough medical examination then took me to a farm in the Gleniffer Braes.

We lived in dormitories and, after a month or so, he asked me if I would like to go to Canada.

But I was a bit scared about going away so far with no chance of getting back home if I didn't like it, especially after all the reports I had received about others being treated like slaves.

So I opted for farm work in Scotland and found a lot of truth in the slavery bit. But I once worked on an MP's farm and it was class.'

These letters were obviously written from heartfelt experience, perhaps a little tremulous and with a certain amount of anger. Their contents are entirely believable.

I hardly knew where to begin. I had never heard of any such schemes outside wartime and found the idea horrifying; as the child of a single parent living in Keppochhill Road I could have been more than eligible for arbitrary removal. Asking a boy who has never been further from Glasgow than the Gleniffer Braes if he would like to go to Canada is like asking if he would like to visit Mars. He could have little or nothing to base his judgment on, far less an answer.

For no reason other than her innocently hopeful ending, I would like to assure Mrs Docherty things were as she suggests. Certainly, I could find no such schemes operating now; changes in the law have prevented that; but it is sobering to think that the last change necessary to ensure the safety of children in care was only enacted in 1982. The unwillingness of our former colonies to take more immigrants, rather than any official concern, caused the scheme's demise. The local authority care as part of the welfare state largely removed children from the sort of private institutions which encouraged most of the emigration. Some even specialised in moving children to what used to be the empire, making room for more unfortunates at home. Before 1982 private Voluntary Institutions did not need to request the permission of the Secretary of State to send children abroad, which often meant they did it without anyone's permission, government official, parent or child.

As everyone knows, welfare care is now diminishing. Contributions to charities are rising and these same charities are once again being encouraged to play their part in helping the deprived of the community achieve a better standard of living. The conditions necessary for the exportation of children are beginning to return.

We have destitute people living on the streets. Care in the community has left many bewildered souls unprotected outside the only homes they have ever known. And as the recent Government instructions to remove the homeless from the streets of London into temporary shelters, rather than attack the cause of them being there in the first place, show, homeless folk wandering the streets are embarrassing and potentially dangerous to the bourgeois eye.

I could find little public reference to the scheme Mr Docherty endured. Nor was there much about Dr Cossar, though he was almost certainly one of a number of well intentioned child exporters. I suspect a trawl of district council or regional council archives would bear fruit: eleven per cent of Canada's population is descended directly from exported children.

The immediate starting point therefore had to be national. The Child Migrants Trust was founded in 1987. It is a registered charity founded to provide specialised and qualified support for former child migrants, their parents and relatives. They are contactable at 8 Kingston Road, West Bridgford, Nottingham NG2 7AQ.

There is little reason to believe that the people who sent children to green fields and fresh air were acting from anything other than what they believed to be the best of motives. Yet the fact remains that the material needs of working class children were, and in some quarters still are, regarded as more important than their emotional needs; and material often means middle class. For generations these children have suffered from a lack of imagination on the part of others who thought they were acting for the best, giving the kids a helping hand, a decent start in life, and sowing the seeds of British culture abroad.

The colonies, especially Australia and Canada, were always seen as an ideal place for political agitators and criminals. In the main, they went

WHAT EMIGRATION IS DOING

By Dr. G. C. COSSAR
(Calton)

I am glad to say that my scheme for training city girls in the rudiments of house-keeping and cookery in farm houses, with a view to fitting them eventually to go over-seas if they so desire, is now further advanced

Following an advertisement there were 19 applications for girls from farmers' wives and within the last two weeks 24 girls have applied to me for posts. Eight of them have been definitely placed and more would have been sent away had it not been for the railway strike.

The girls' fares are paid by the farmers' and they get from six shillings per week upwards and board according to age.

A Glasgow girl whose fare to Canada I advanced some years ago at the request of her brother, whom I had previously sent out, went on to a farm as a domestic help in her new country. She married a young Canadian and, largely through her own strength of character, they have now a motor-boat and motor-car hiring establishment, a soft-drink parlour and a handsome hotel. That girl would have had no chance here, but in the new land there was room for her to rise as there is for all who care to follow her example.

Miss Irwin, of the Scottish Women's Industrial Council, is co-operating with me in my scheme. She is taking much trouble in seeing the girls, sending them away and, in special cases, getting the necessary clothes for those who are badly off.

Two weeks ago I had an interview with the Juvenile Department of the Ministry of Labour in London and found the officials very sympathetic. I hope that some of the Juvenile Advisory Committee's in England and Scotland will take up the matter energetically.

———:o:———

Article by Dr Cossar in the *Glasgow Eastern Standard*
2 February 1924

voluntarily to Canada and were transported to Australia. Both places were sufficiently far away for society to forget about them and to ensure they could only return to this country with difficulty. The antipodean talent for soap opera gives the original immigrants' descendants an opportunity for minor acts of revenge.

Both countries became the natural destination for displaced children. The economics were entirely favourable. In the 19th century it cost around £12 a year to keep a child in a home. A one-way ticket to Canada or Australia would cost around £15; even when a child's meagre luggage is taken into account, it made financial sense.

The absence of laws protecting destitute children made it entirely possible for homes, which operated with little or no state regulation, to send children abroad without their parents' wishes or knowledge. Notification of this possibility may have been hidden in the small print of whatever document the parent signed, or marked, on surrendering the child into charitable care.

Not only were parents seldom informed of their child's removal, but the children were often told their natural parents had died, supposedly to prevent any emotional difficulties they might find in adjusting to their new lives. Some were told they were going away for a short holiday and would return home in a few weeks. Brothers and sisters were often separated on arrival and might never meet again.

Though their circumstances could be seen as taking on the habits of a Shakespeare comedy or a Dickens tragedy, reality often found the majority of the emigrants unprepared for their new environments. Children, who largely came from urban backgrounds, were sent into the country; on arrival they were expected to have skills from baking to bricklaying which they had never been taught. These children were separated from everything they had known, then transported into the loneliest situations possible. The Australian outback or the Canadian wheatfields bred small, insular communities as different from city streets as it is possible to be; and these communities often did not welcome 'home children'.

Even William Quarrier, the Glaswegian child welfare activist, who prepared his little emigrants by teaching them farming and household crafts, sent boys to Canada equipped with three suits, four shirts, four pairs of socks, a box of collars, boots, a copy of *Pilgrim's Progress*, a Bible and a pocket knife. There were neither coats nor bonnets, scarves nor gloves for Canada's sub-zero winters.

It would be comforting to believe the children were well received into kindly families, but there was little or no scrutinisation of their ultimate destinations. At best there would be a cursory examination of references and a potential foster parent would have to sign an optimistic undertaking which was almost impossible to enforce. Even where the emigration agencies attempted to keep a check on their charges, time, distance and numbers made it impossible.

Quarrier appointed a Visitor to ensure the children were being well looked after, nourished and educated, but conditions were far from ideal. For example, in 1892 Alexander Burges, who was Quarrier's Visitor for the whole of Canada, had 3000 children to visit. He made it to 2000, but each child was seen only once in the year. Foster parents could ensure children were unavailable for interview or they might be warned in advance of the Visitor's arrival. Almost inevitably, threats were used to encourage children to pretend all was well. Quarrier visited his Canadian project in 1888. He saw 300 children. 'It would be difficult to describe the comfortable homes and favourable circumstances in which we found the children,' he wrote later.

Emigrants were sent abroad for their own self improvement, though some were more in need than others. There was a near mutiny aboard the *Earl Gray*, bound for the colonies in 1847, when the 53 girls who arrived on board in their new bonnets, dresses and little hand cases, turned out to be teenage prostitutes from Marylebone.

Emigration was also used as a means of social control and the criminality of some children who were sent over generally gave home children a bad reputation. Then as now, both the children and sections of the general public tended to believe they were in care because they had done something wrong.

This must have affected the way the children were treated, though the risk of them being used as slave labour was inevitably high and an endemic part of the system. The children working on what amounted to communal farms seem to have been even more exposed to financial and physical exploitation. There are many examples, ranging from a Quarrier girl, sent to Ontario in 1889, who was given three days in solitary confinement and a severe beating for being unable to eat rice pudding, to the systematic physical and sexual abuse carried out by the Christian Brothers at the Bindoon Boys Town, near Perth, Australia. Little more than 30 years ago at least six boys were abused to such an extent they needed corrective surgery.

When it became unavoidably obvious that sexual abuse was taking place, Annie MacPherson, who ran a child emigrant scheme and who first encouraged William Quarrier to become involved in child emigration, tried to circumvent the problem by exporting only very young children.

Quarrier was careful to put boys under the charge of married couples and girls in the care of single women in his Bridge of Weir village, yet curiously neither his, nor any other, emigration agency was particularly scrupulous about the situations of their former charges overseas.

Neither was it always obvious to the children that they were free to leave their new homes when they came of age. Robbed of their dignity and roots, the youngsters were often relieved of their wages, as well as the clothing they had brought with them. Dotheboys Hall springs unbidden to the mind as money, which was supposedly kept in trust, disappeared into institutional coffers. Without money, or any idea of themselves as independent human beings, the children were often worse off than those who stayed in institutions, even though they were liable to find themselves on the streets when they came of age and state support for their care was terminated.

William Quarrier was Glasgow's leading child exporter. From relatively modest beginnings in 1864, he helped thousands of destitute children, who otherwise would have died on the streets, find shelter, safety, health and fulfilment. His Industrial Brigades provided food, clothing and employment. His city homes and shelters eventually gave rise to the Bridge of Weir Village, which was built to receive boys and girls in an atmosphere of proper education, training and growth.

By modern standards, Quarrier's methods seem a little crude. Girls were largely trained to be maidservants, wives and mothers, boys became little farmhands and labourers. As a self-made man, he had a fairly limited view of the path to success. Hard work and Christian fortitude were strongly emphasised.

Quarrier highlighted a problem his contemporaries had ignored and he obviously saved very many young lives. Unfortunately, the same faith which, to this day, has meant Quarrier's Homes leave their fund raising entirely in the hands of God and their good reputation, also lent a rosy glow to child emigration. When the first of Quarrier's child migrants set sail on 2 July 1872, he genuinely believed they were bound for a better life. Canada's strong Scottish connections led him to view the country as a kind of Caledonian colony, friendly and rich in opportunities for self improvement.

That he was naively wrong is testified by Andrew Doyle's report to the Local Government Board in 1875. Doyle had been asked to investigate child immigration to Canada from Britain because of disturbing rumours which had filtered back to the board's attention. They also supplied children to immigration schemes.

Doyle found the children insufficiently protected, the destitute were exported along with the criminal, insufficient inspection visits were carried out, the entire scheme was poorly organised and badly administered. Such abuses were widespread.

Annie MacPherson's receiving homes in Ontario, which took all of

Quarrier's early Glaswegian exports, were excluded from the most damning criticism. The report described her as a 'true and disinterested benefactor' and Agnes Bilbrough, who was in charge of MacPherson's Marchmont Home in Ontario, was even more highly praised for her personal devotion to duty. Criticism was reserved for Maria Rye, who exported 4000 to Canada with a criminal lack of concern for their well being. MacPherson and Rye had been sanctioned by the Local Government Board and so came under their direct scrutiny.

Despite Doyle's comments, Annie MacPherson effectively closed her operations for two years in an attempt to implement many of the report's recommendations. And though the Doyle report caused considerable public concern, neither the British nor the Canadian governments took any action until 1897 when Ontario brought in the Act to Regulate the Immigration into Ontario of Certain Classes of Children, which protected child immigrants up to the age of 18.

When William Quarrier found he could not send children to Ontario on the terms he was used to, he refused to send them at all, finding the regulations an insult to his care. Emigration began again in 1904 after Quarrier's death.

It is difficult not to embrace the unpalatable notion that sometimes those we believed to be good guys, were maybe not so. Ignorance is no excuse in law, nor, I suspect, in the Docherty household.

WORKS CONSULTED:
Kenneth Bagnell, *The Little Immigrants* (Macmillan of Canada, 1980).
Philip Bean and Joy Melville, *Lost Children of the Empire* (Unwin, 1989).
Anna Magnusson, *The Village: a History of Quarrier's Homes* (Quarrier's Homes, 1984).
J. Rose, *For the Sake of the Children* (Hodder and Stoughton, 1987).
John Urquhart, *The Life Story of William Quarrier* (R. L. Allan and Son, 1901).
Gillian Wagner, *Children of the Empire* (Weidenfeld and Nicolson, 1982).
Children at Risk (Strathclyde Regional Council, 1987).
Home or Away (Strathclyde Regional Council, 1983).

ARCHITECTURE AND THE GLASGOWS OF THE IMAGINATION

CHARLES McKEAN

ARCHITECTURE IS the memory of a city: but it is not necessarily the sole memory of it. What distinguishes the *architectural* memory is its reality. The memory can be measured, tested and analysed for what it tells us about the people who paid for it, who created it and who used it. Buildings have always been relatively expensive in time, labour or cash, and thus record what each generation considered its priorities. What people built, why they built and how well they built it represents social history in stone.

Architecture becomes peculiarly important as an historical anchor whilst a city develops its images and its myths — as all cities do; (occasionally, indeed, cities become more mythical than real, and symbolic more of states of mind and the human condition than of history). As reality recedes, amnesia develops, and the city becomes chymerical. Babylon is one such city; Glasgow has become another.

The world's images of Glasgow are the creation of vivid imaginations supported by selective interpretation and exhibition. Although these 'Glasgows of the mind' may well be explicable by the fact that the reality of much 19th and 20th century Glasgow was so horrendous that the only artistic escape was itself cerebral, the city is unusual in the high level of creative activity which it fostered when taken against similar industrial cities like Hamburg, Rotterdam, Clermont Ferrand or Detroit. Perhaps the artistic output of Glasgow may be taken to speak for all industrial cities (a somewhat extravagant claim when taken against Sinclair Lewis, Orwell or Zola). But 20th century novels and plays have focused upon limited aspects at the expense of the rest. In war, after all (and Glasgow has enjoyed its role in class warfare), the first casualty is truth.

Thus it was that the preferred image of Glasgow became that of a Victorian Babylon: the *Cancer of Empire*, the Glasgow of adversity, of *No Mean City* and *The Shipbuilders*, of the Gorbals and Red Clydeside, and of single-ends, slums and exploited underdogs. Artists, poets, authors and photographers duly captured that image (for it was not hard to find) and supporting documentation was soon created. The image acquired a substantial supporting constituency. Its momentum was inexorable, and the myth became self perpetuating.

It also suited the Stalinists of the post-1945 period to be able to dismiss the achievements of Victorian Glasgow as evil and exploitative; for it inhibited objections to the implementation of their grand plans — initially to redevelop the entire city centre and, from 1958, to raze utterly the thousands of acres of Inner Glasgow and obliterate its memory. At one point, as Anderston Cross, after Charing Cross, after St George's Cross, after Cowcaddens was crushed beneath concrete, it seemed as though they would be successful.

Perhaps because the middle classes had been fleeing the city for at least 100 years, opposition to this fundamentally working class perspective was flaccid. Those buttressed in Bearsden were disengaged in the battle for Glasgow's soul. Their social credentials were now insufficient: nobody born outside a tenement flat was deemed capable of a correct view on the matter; and the rump of the liberal middle classes who, marooned in Novar Drive, still retained such credentials, was soon routed. Glasgow's history became overwhelmed by an enormous guilt complex.

Literature was little help. Fiction, with the rare exception of Guy McCrone's *Wax Fruit*, spurned the restless, pushy, clever, innovative and exploitative Highlander-turned-entrepreneurs who were largely the creators of Glasgow's wealth and status, and its elevation to a world power. Nor have the city's history books been much better, until very recently. Overburdened by the guilt complex, they have misunderstood and apologised for the Victorian achievements, and relegated anything earlier to a picturesque aberration: a city of funny little men in red cloaks called Tobacco Lords, and eccentrics like the wall-eyed Bob Dragon (otherwise Robert Dreghorn of Ruchill and possibly as powerful a man in his day as Jimmy Gulliver is in ours). In short, the authorised version of Glasgow's history, earning the *imprimatur* of the literati, may be summarised thus: pre-Victorian Glasgow is not really serious; Victorian and Edwardian Glasgow was on balance a bad thing, but distinguished by the people's and the unions' struggle; and the task of 20th century Glasgow is to shake off the shackles of the past to produce a new Utopia.

This mythological Glasgow bred subsidiary myths. The exploitative Glaswegians were also philistines. Did they not, after all, drive Charles Rennie Mackintosh unloved and poverty-struck from their city? As it happens, they did not. The exuberant artistic patronage that created the McLellan Galleries, Kelvingrove, the finest concert hall in Europe in the St Andrew's Halls and patronised the Glasgow Boys, also patronised Mackintosh whilst the economy boomed (although the pragmatism of the city was ill matched with Mackintosh's perfectionism). The city's economy had collapsed by 1910, and it was clear to Mackintosh that there was little possibility of his ever again receiving a commission of the importance and scale of his masterwork, the School of Art. Aged 45 in 1913, the time had come to quit Glasgow — *and architecture* — to resume his first love of painting.

In the early 1980s, a new generation of Glaswegians, untrammelled by that guilty conscience, and heavily involved in the regeneration and cleaning of the city, sensed that the depressed Glasgow so beloved of photo journalists was a partial view; and in ignorance of the city's real history, sought to present a new perception: hence 'Glasgow's Miles Better'. But better than what? They had no other resources upon which to draw. They had forgotten the memory of the city. Their 'better' was solely better than the guilty conscience would admit: no more, no less. *That* is the depths to which our collective amnesia had dragged us. Predictably, the cheery glitz of the 'Miles Better' campaigners stood little chance against the dour, Calvinist, masochistically-enjoyed misery of a history of oppression, unemployment drunkenness, macho behaviour and aggression. 'Oot o' the east, there came a hard man . . .', and they still flattered him as the custodian of the city's soul.

Other Glasgows of the mind — particularly television programmes like *Tutti Frutti* and *Taggart* — not so much reversed the hard image as added new ingredients to the cocktail, like fashionable restaurants, glossy hotels, bars and cafés, and a new breed of anti-heroes: Glaswegians on the make. Although the City of Culture programme has made an enormous dunt in the Stalinist mono-cultural conception of Glasgow, maybe even dealing it a mortal wound, it came as little surprise that the exhibition which sought to encapsulate the richness and variety of Glasgow's competing histories and cultures — *Glasgow's Glasgow* — should be vilified and picketed largely on the grounds that the oppressed Glasgow, on which so much artistic invention had fed, was being both psychologically and physically peripheralised by a new, vigorously emerging city.

The Glasgows of the imagination exist in their own right. But it is remarkable that the city has so neglected and misunderstood the reality of its own history: and that is what its architecture has to tell us.

Interpreting Glasgow's history from its architecture presents a particular difficulty as a consequence of the city's fondness for rebuilding itself. Virtually all of the extensive mediaeval, stone-built archiepiscopal community, with its Vicars' Close, Prebendaries' dwellings, charitable hospitals and imposingly fortified palace has vanished with the overwhelmed exception of the Provand's Lordship and the Cathedral itself. All — with the exception of the Tolbooth Steeple (shorn of the magnificent 17th century civic monument that gave it meaning) — of the boom town of 17th century Scotland has vanished. No less grievous losses include Scotland's finest 17th century university, the Netherlandish Merchants' House in the Briggait, Hutchesons' Hospital in the Trongate, a number of elaborate and wealthy mercantile dwellings enjoying 'a' the comforts o' the Sautmarket'; and — above all — the four great streets of arcaded tenements built upon the Continental model after the horrendous fire of 1652 had destroyed most of the Saltmarket, Trongate, Gallowgate and High Street. These streets attracted the admiration of all visitors until their removal from c.1820 onwards.

Of Tobacco Lord Glasgow — that quaintly portrayed slice of Glaswegian history that is as significant in understanding the city's culture and achievements as any other period — there remains but one restored villa in Charlotte Street and a mutilated clone in Miller Street. Yet this was the city that acted as the primary American tobacco landfall for Britain if not Europe; whose merchants' houses shared common characteristics with those of their trading partners in Virginia, Annapolis and other places on the American eastern seaboard, producing an architecture and building form virtually unique in Europe. This was the city of such wealth (even though coin was short) that a French visitor noticed with amazement that the new Palladian villas of the Tobacco Lords were not just pedimented with carved urns, but that their windows *were gilded on the outside*. One such Tobacco Lord, John Glassford of Dougalston, was said by a contemporary to have earned £500,000 sterling in 1772; at an equivalent of at least £300 million today, he must have been one of the richest commoners in Europe.

These energetic people caused the Clyde to be dredged up to Glasgow, caused Port Glasgow to be constructed, and caused Smeaton to build the Forth and Clyde Canal. The silly notion of picturesque eccentrics withers in the light of their achievements. It is even more inappropriate a view of their 17th century predecessors, who seized power from the Bishops and nobility, shifted the balance of the town downhill, and built a new civic church, charitable hospital, Guildhall, and the most splendid Tolbooth and University in 17th century Scotland. The restless, pushy, innovative entrepreneur as the core of Glasgow's success can be observed 200 years before the creation of Park Circus and Beardmore's Forge; just as he has emerged again today (a wonderfully twisted version of whom appeared as the glorious Mr Clockerty in *Tutti Frutti*). From the 16th to the 20th century (with an added melancholy once the city absorbs its preponderant Celtic population from the Highlands and Ireland in the 19th) their characteristics remain consistent: an intense drive matched with canniness, a disregard for any establishment save their own, and an almost pathological objection to civic action until there was no choice; and thereafter civic intervention with the same heedless drive that had been applied to mercantile expansion.

The 16th century Italian architect Jacopo Sansovino once wrote that a city does not lie in great buildings, streets and monuments, but in people making the most of their opportunity. Yet the proof of their activities, the proof of this other Glasgow, this real Glasgow, this optimistic if opportunistic Glasgow, does indeed lie in the great streets and monuments which they bequeathed to us; and that proof can be retrieved by study of what they built from old paintings and drawings. Until the full treasures held by the city's museums are disgorged (and it is odd that they are not) it is to the Mitchell Library's Glasgow Room and its genial staff that we must go to excavate a true corrective to the Glasgows of the mind. It helps if you know in advance what you are looking for, (although there is no joy greater than serendipity — the chancing upon something unexpected); and there are a number of totem buildings from Glasgow's mercantile history of quite exceptional importance of which no visual record has yet been unearthed.

The first is the great tenement built in the Saltmarket by Sir William Bruce for the merchant Provost William Gibson in 1677. Bruce was then Scotland's greatest architect, and no other town residence (for Holyrood Palace hardly qualifies as such) by Bruce is known. According to Glasgow's first historian John McUre, Gibson's Land was 'admir'd by all forreigners and strangers', having four arches leading into a courtyard, and a facade decorated with the several orders of architecture. The setting for Tobias Smollett's *Roderick Random*, it collapsed in 1823. With luck, therefore, there may yet be found a drawing of the west side of Saltmarket prior to 1823 which will reveal the building. It might also — and would that it did — reveal something of the building on the corner of Saltmarket and the Trongate, fleetingly glimpsed in Robert Paul's 1760s drawing of the latter. There is a tantalising indication of a two-storeyed oriel window corbelled out from the corner in a quite splendid example of a Scottish Renaissance detail we know better from drawings of Cardinal Beaton's house in Edinburgh's Cowgate.

The next mysterious monument requiring rediscovery is the house of Daniel Campbell of Shawfield MP, erected in 1711 to face axially down Stockwell Street to designs by the Glasgow lawyer Colen Campbell. Campbell subsequently went on to become the *doyen* of English Palladian Architecture with the publication of *Vitruvius Britannicus* from which volume the only illustration of the Shawfield Mansion is known. He was also responsible for the designs of some of the totems of Palladianism such as Mereworth Castle in Kent. It defies belief that a building so grandiose and so central, the residence of Bonnie Prince Charlie when courting Clementina Walkinshaw, and the home of Glassford of Douglaston, should have formed no part of anyone's drawing or sketch prior to its removal for the construction of Glassford Street in 1791. The People's Palace painting of Glassford and his family implies, in somewhat naive style, a walled rear garden with brick gazebo, and a view into a narrow adjacent street.

In 1756, Provost Buchanan attempted to outdo the Shawfield Mansion by the construction of the even more magnificent Virginia Mansion which faced down Virginia Street. Considered the 'most stately mansion in the whole of the city' it became the home of Alexander Spiers of Elderslie, merchant, entrepreneur, mill owner, and one of the four young men of talent to whose exertions Glasgow owed its late 18th century prosperity, according to Provost Cochrane. Of this princely house is known to exist only an out-of-scale drawing of little evidential and no artistic value.

Cotton town Glasgow, which succeeded Tobacco Lord Glasgow after the American Revolution in 1775, imported Robert and James Adam. None of the great civic enterprises which Edinburgh offered to them — such as Charlotte Square or the University — came their way in Glasgow: for in Glasgow civic enterprise was subsumed to private or quasi private enterprise. That they designed the Athenaeum, the Infirmary and the Trades House is well known, although the curious location of the Infirmary has never been fully appreciated. It was possibly the first new building in the Upper town for 150 years, its scale dwarfing the crumbled ecclesiastic buildings now occupied by mechanics. Its location was determined by the Upper Town's distance from Glasgow, and its salubrious air (long before the pollutions of the infamous St Rollox Works). Exactly converse reasons explain why the Trades quit their Upper Town location in the Parsonage of Morebattle, at about the same time, for their smart new Adam-designed Hall closing the vista down Garth Street. An Upper Town location was no longer sufficient for the 'increasing respectability of the Trades Rank'.

It is now known that the Adam brothers designed a Corn Exchange for the head of College Street, the vista flanked by the only two completed parts of the scheme — two blocks of Professors houses, in one of which Dr William Hunter established his first Hunterian Museum. (They vanished before the proposed East Flank motorway in the 1970s). The Adam brothers proposed entire palace blocks for George Square and for Ingram Street (neither completed) and an extraordinary Tron Kirk for the Trongate, its classical, pedimented front flanked by shops. It is said, but remains unproven, that Robert Adam also designed Charlotte Street. The most extraordinary proposal, however, for which no illustration appears to survive save the architects' own drawings, was Stirling's Square, to the west of the High Street. This 'queer out of the way sort of place, a sort of aneurism on South Albion Street' was never completed because of Stirling's failure to buy all the necessary properties. But much was built, of which Babbity Bowster's in Blackfriars Street is an isolated relic. These buildings are unique in the Adam canon being formal palace-fronted blocks similar to Edinburgh's Charlotte Square, but consisting not of terraced houses but tenement flats above warehouses and shops. Survives there yet a drawing of Stirling's Square?

Equally sparse, now that we know that we are looking for them, are views of Glasgow's New Town in the first flush of youth — that recorded by Dorothy Wordsworth: 'built of fine stone in the best style of the very best London streets but, not being of brick, they are greatly superior'. Only recently has it been understood how unusual the New Town or Merchant City really is. It not only exemplified the city's consistent opposition to civic action by throwing any development therein to the mercies of private enterprise and speculation; but it also illustrated a confoundedly pragmatic or *ad-hoc* attitude. None of Edinburgh's master plan, Edinburgh's feu conditions, Edinburgh's land ownership. The site for Glasgow's New Town was sprinkled with ancient routes, Tobacco Lord villas, recent houses and the Ramshorn Kirk. Glasgow accepted these old tracks and new houses as fixed, and wove them into an initially ramshackle cotton town, gradually turning what had been a disadvantage into an asset. The fact that Ingram Street was closed to the west by the Cunninghame Mansion (later transformed into a Royal Exchange) and the Candleriggs to the north by the Ramshorn became the *leitmotif* of what followed: Hutcheson Street closed by Hutchesons Hospital, Glassford Street by the Star Inn, Garth Street to the east by the Merchants' and to the west by the Trades' Hall, Buchanan Street by St Enoch's Church and George Street by St George's Tron.

The valuable drawings of Robert Carrick of the 1850s do not catch the essence of the earlier town before the merchants quit for new houses in Blythswood Hill; nor do the beautiful but formalised drawings of Joseph Swan, for illustrations of that period concentrated more upon monuments. A fleeting glimpse of Glassford Street in the *Chronicles of Gotham* reveals majestic buildings sitting upon huge rusticated arcades of a Roman majesty: and something of the sort is implied in James Denholm's 1798 figurative drawing of the same street. But is there nothing else? For this is the bustling, enterprising city of cotton merchants, the Glasgow of the clubs as Dr John Strang had it: the last time the city could be called an integrated community with all classes living in proximity.

Last, but far from least in this search for architectural triggers to the understanding of Glasgow's past, is the strange case of Alexander 'Picture' Gordon's house at 53 Buchanan Street. Just as other mercantile princes had brought in the services of the Adam brothers, Gordon went to London to purchase the services of Sir John Soane, perhaps the most distinguished and certainly most distinctive architect in Europe of his time, for his 'elegant mansion', the gardens of which extended behind into Royal Exchange Square.

The vista to the front of his new picture palace Gordon preserved by buying the land for Gordon Street (which is otherwise an aberration in the Glasgow grid). Gordon, the first of Glasgow's great art collectors, had constructed his new house — Soane's *only* town house in Britain save his own in Lincoln's Inns Fields in London — in 1804 to house his pictures. The only known illustration is the 1842 street elevation of Buchanan Street as a whole, which implies a flat roofed, pilastered two-storeyed facade with some visual similarities to Pitshanger Manor in London.

In almost any other city, the presence of a Soane building would have been treasured like the presence of a Titian or Van Gogh. Not only is its presence generally *not* known but, once again, its appearance does not yet seem to have been recorded. Somewhere, it will have been.

These examples exemplify how old paintings, sketches, plans, maps and even doodles, such as those in archives or the Glasgow Room in the Mitchell Library, can be essential to the excavation and understanding of social aspiration and change as recorded in buildings. Architecture, both surviving and demolished, provides a real history of the city and a corrective to the creations of the imagination. It does indeed represent the memory of Glasgow.

GLASGOW AT LEISURE, 1850

ADAM McNAUGHTAN

THE 1850s was a decade of decision in Glasgow. Already in the first half of the century the council had stepped in to provide work for the unemployed, levelling and draining the Green, quarrying stone for the extension of the harbour for a River Clyde deepened at the council's direction, but it was in this decade that there began the wide-ranging intervention which was to make Glasgow a world model for municipal organisation. To the massive financial burden involved in taking over and improving the city's water supply was added the cost of providing parks in the west end and south side, only partially offset by feuing adjacent property, and the first venture at a city art gallery when it was decided to purchase the Sauchiehall Street building which housed the McLellan bequest of 400 pictures.

In 1850 municipal optimism was high. The triumph of the previous year's royal visit had erased the memory of the 1848 cholera epidemic and Bread Riots. The prospect for Glasgow's employers must have seemed cloudless. The textile industries were thriving; Glasgow was spinning 45 million pounds of cotton per year. The financial crises of the late 50s, which were to leave the industry unable to bear the American War's interruption, cast no shadow before. Shipping and ship-building on the still-deepening river were booming. Sixty-seven iron ships were built on the Clyde in the five years to 1850. The rapid growth in population — from 270,000 in 1841 to 333,000 in 1851 — meant that labour was plentiful and cheap.

For the classes who supplied that labour things were not so rosy. The remaining hand-loom weavers were earning 15 per cent less than they had earned a decade before. Unemployment was a constant threat and emigration an attraction. Hours were long. The Early Closing movement sought to persuade shopkeepers to close by seven o'clock on weekdays and five o'clock on Saturdays. In 1850 many establishments still remained open until eight or nine o'clock six days a week. For the working classes leisure time was short and precious.

That time would seldom be spent in the small, ill-ventilated, overcrowded home; it might be spent in a small, ill-ventilated, overcrowded spirit-shop. There was no shortage of these, as the City Chamberlain, John Strang, was forced to admit to the British Association that year, though he argued that Glasgow's drink consumption was no worse than that of English cities. Neither Trongate nor Saltmarket is very long, but they boasted between them 70 licensed taverns or spirit dealers. Indeed, the town only had to provide four

Prince's Theatre-Royal.

HAPPY NEW-YEAR TO ALL.

FIRST PRICE. ... BOXES, 3s.; ... STALLS, 2s. 6d.; ... PIT, 1s. 6d.; ... GALLERY, 6d.
SECOND PRICE. .... BOXES, 2s.; .... STALLS, 1s. 6d.; .... PIT, 1s.; .... No Second Price to Gallery.
SECOND PRICE at NINE o'clock. The Performances to terminate as near as possible at a Quarter past 11.
DOORS WILL OPEN AT SEVEN—THE CURTAIN TO RISE AT HALF-PAST SEVEN.

In reply to several anonymous Letters, Mr GLOVER begs to state that he is averse to all personal and local allusions in a Pantomime, as these are certain to give offence in some quarter; and as to 'Means and Substance,' Poor's Rates, &c., he humbly thinks people have more than enough of them at home.

Mr GLOVER has great pleasure in announcing the most TRIUMPHANT SUCCESS in the NEW COMIC PANTOMIME that ever was achieved in Glasgow. It having been hailed throughout with the most enthusiastic applause and shouts of laughter, he feels justified in announcing its Repetition Every Evening until further Notice.

MORNING PERFORMANCE
THIS DAY
OF THE SPLENDID PANTOMIME OF
OLD MOTHER SHIPTON:
AT HALF-PAST ONE O'CLOCK. The Theatre will be Illuminated with Gas.
MORNING PRICES :—Boxes, 2s.; Stalls, 1s. 6d.; Pit, 1s.; Gallery, 6d.

This Evening, TUESDAY, 1st Jan., 1850,
The Performances to commence with the Comedietta of

FAINT HEART NEVER WON FAIR LADY
The Duchess de Terreneuva by Miss ROSA BENNETT   Donna Leonora, her Aunt, by Miss MARRIOTT
Charles II. King of Spain, aged 15, by Mrs MARSHALL   Ruy Gomez by Mr DAVID FISHER   Marquis de Santa Cruz, Governor of the King, by Mr MORGAN
Lopez by Mr H. WALTON

Previous to the Pantomime, will be Exhibited

BOUGH'S GRAND MOVING PANORAMA
REPRESENTING THE QUEEN'S VISIT TO GLASGOW.
From Views taken as near the spot as circumstances would allow him to go,
Her Majesty's Departure from Belfast in the Fairy Yacht—Putting out to sea—Passing the Royal Squadron—Firing a salute—Sunset off the Irish Coast—Streak gulls in the offing—Heavy weather coming on—The gallant craft riding o'er the billows.
Tempest themselves, high seas and howling winds, | Do quit their common nature, letting go safely by | The beloved VICTORIA.—(Shakspere.)
GOD SAVE THE QUEEN.
Loch-Ryan—Entering the Clyde—DUMBARTON CASTLE—Morning—LANDING OF THE QUEEN—Glorious Welcome and unsurpassed Preparations of the Loyal Citizens.

TRIUMPHAL ARCH & ANIMATED SCENE at the OLD CATHEDRAL,
From the celebrated Lithographs published by Maclure and Macdonald.

COMIC SONG. ... ... **by Mr S. COWELL.**
GRAND PAS DE DEUX ... ... **by Madlle. ADELE and M. MARTIN.**

To be followed by the laughable Farce of

THE LITTLE BACK PARLOUR
Mrs Simon Stubbs by Mrs C. F. MARSHALL   Miss Lucy Baggens by Miss CLARA WYNNE
Mr Simon Stubbs by Mr C. F. MARSHALL   Mr Snooks by Mr MORGAN   Billy Blue by Mr H. WALTON

After which will be produced, a New and Splendid Grand Comic Pantomime,
Which has been some months in preparation, and for which the best talent in every department has been secured, regardless of a vast expense, it being the earnest desire of the Management to present a Pantomime fully equal to anything ever acted in this City, the title of which is,

OLD MOTHER SHIPTON AND HER CAT;
Or, HARLEQUIN SIR RIQUET WITH THE TUFT.
With entire New Scenery, Music, Dresses, Decorations, Properties, Tricks, Masks, Transformations and Incantations, Dances, Choruses, and Comic Songs.
THE BUSINESS OF THE COMIC SCENES ARRANGED BY MR PARRY.
The whole produced under the entire Direction of Mr EDMUND GLOVER.

CHARACTERS IN TH'S OPENING.
Mother Shipton (an Old Lady that sails in the air when the moon shines fair,) by Mr C. F. MARSHALL   Greymalkin (her favourite Cat,) by Signor BERNARSKINI
Chanticleer (This is the cock that crow'd in the morn,) by Master COCK-O-DOODLE-DOO
The haughty Indivious Madingara coodlemacoodle (an individual with more head than heart,) by Mr WALTON
Elspeth Meacoodle (A charming rose, with mother's eyes and father's nose,) by Mr DANVERS
Ellenstar (the Cinderella of the Family, afterward Columbine,) by Miss SUSAN MASSALL
Peasant Girls, Housemaids, &c. &c.
Peachblossom (Queen of the Fairies,) by Mrs C. F. MARSHALL
Zephyr, Starlight, Twilight, Sunbeam, Lightfoot, Cowslip, Cobweb, Goldlocks, Dewdrop, Maybud, Waterbubble, and Brighteye, attendant Fairies, by the Ladies of the Ballet
Sir Riquet with the Tuft (a Dwarf Knight, most kind, though crook'd in body, yet noble in mind,) by Master BECKETT
Cullender Kitchenerpan (Head Cook of the Magic Kitchen,) by Mr BECKETT
Too many Cooks by a tasty, well-dressed set of Scupers
Turnspits of the Magic Kitchen by Ten Young Gentlemen, engaged expressly for this occasion, with the full sanction and approbation of their Parents—by Masters Frish, Dash, Toby, Quilp, Mouse, Bengo, Rover, Pincher, and Poodle   Retainers of the Baroness, Villagers, Invisible Chorus, &c.

TRANSFORMATION.
Columbine................by Miss SUSAN MASSALL | Clown.....................................by Mr G. PARRY
Harlequin................by M. VERONI | Pantaloon.........................by CARLO BOLENO
Pierrott...................by Signor BERNASKINI

For a Description of the Sixteen Splendid New Scenes and Comicality of the Pantomime, see Double Bill.
BOOKS, with the Words, Choruses, Songs, &c., and a full Description of the Pantomime; also, a LITHOGRAPHIC KEY to BOUGH'S GRAND PANORAMA of the QUEEN'S VISIT, to be had at the Doors of the Theatre, price THREEPENCE.

street lamps in Saltmarket, so many of the pubs had their own pavement lights.

Then, as now, there were some pubs whose sole purpose was the sale and consumption of drink, where the working men crowded in to drab premises, paid their money and downed their drams. Other taverns, however, developed a character of their own and attracted a particular clientele. So racing men, such as the ironmaster, James Merry, or Sir William Don, Britain's best-known amateur actor, found their way to Buchanan's in the French Horn close, 88 Trongate. Before the Forbes-Mackenzie Act came into force in 1854, there was little control over opening hours, and Norman Buchanan's was one of several houses which opened from six in the evening to six or eight the following morning. As the address suggests, there was another tavern, The French Horn, in the same close. This was no uncommon occurrence. Several of the closes in Trongate and Saltmarket housed three or four pubs. At no. 18 Saltmarket were the Waverley, the Three Tuns, the Globe and the Scots Grey. (There were two other Scots Greys in the vicinity.) This Scots Grey was noted as a haunt of military men, being kept by Mrs Scott, widow of a sergeant. In winter she kept a pot of potatoes always on the fender, to relish the dram. The Waverley was run by Mrs Crawford who kept one of the best houses in the city, as recalled 40 years later by a writer in the Weekly Mail:

> Smart waiting-maids attended the customers. The stairs were whitened down every morning, the mahogany handrail polished, and also the brass rods which sparred the glass door. The windows to the front were always kept scrupulously clean with neat white blinds on them.

It was in 1850 that Mrs Crawford purchased a new property in George Square and the Waverley was taken over by another kenspeckle female, Mrs Dupain, who had been managing licensed premises in Mumford's former 'mechanical theatre' at the foot of Saltmarket, in which her husband had once been a performer. Mrs Dupain was to turn the Waverley into one of the district's best singing saloons, but in 1850 the finest of these was the Shakespeare, one stair up at 36 Saltmarket, with a bowling alley on the ground floor. The bowling alley came into its own after midnight when the upstairs rooms closed: cockfighting, dog-fighting and prize-fighting could all take place in the early hours of the morning.

It was, however, as a singing saloon, that the Shakespeare made its reputation. The Saltmarket at one time had eight taverns offering professional entertainment, but in 1850 the Shakespeare and the Jupiter were the leading two. W. G. Ross, by this time a London star with his infamous rendition of

'Sam Hall', had sung here frequently in his early days. A current favourite was David Brown, who had come back to his native Glasgow five years before as a leading tenor at the short-lived City Theatre and who was to play a leading role in the development of Music Hall in Glasgow. At the Jupiter in July 1850 you might have heard 'Miss Coutts, whose characteristic songs are very piquant, Mr Cooke, a skilful performer on the banjo, and Mr Alister McLean, a highland piper and dancer, who appears in both capacities at once, with an effect which it is not easy to describe.' W. F. Frame, writing in 1907, recalled the Jupiter putting on a Christmas pantomime in his early days.

As well as these professional tavern entertainments there were many pubs with rooms set aside for amateurs willing to take their chance in front of a crowd of their peers. A hostile critic described one in the *Abstainers' Journal* of 1854:

> The door opens and our ears are at once regaled with very fine music from a piano and a skilful player at the head of the room, in which are seated about 130 well-dressed lads belonging to various handicrafts in the city. We find ourselves in what is called a 'Free-and-Easy'. Anything but that to us about five minutes to eleven on a Saturday night. About 20 tobacco pipes are puffing away at once; and a pipe force such as this kept constantly going for three or four hours — the reader may easily suppose — has filled the room to such an extent that 'the lights are dimly burning'. The chairman rises (for the company has a president, and one by far too good-looking and well-dressed for such a place) and demands a song from Mr So-and-so. In the meantime the waiter has been getting orders for more drink, and is now busy supplying his customers in various parts of the room, whilst Mr So-and-so is clearing his throat for his song. He sings well and is loudly encored; but eleven o'clock is striking and the company must break up. . . . The publican has done his part well. He has provided excellent music, so far as a good piano and a more than average player is concerned. He has gathered around him a few lads with good voices, and ambitious of being known as singers. One brings another. Drink has been plentifully circulated. The pianist has got a few shillings, and as much drink as he pleases for his night's work, and the publican, on summing up, finds he has made quite a 'hit'. He has discovered that music is an excellent bait. He does not at all object to questionable songs. Not he, 'unless they come it too strong'; and the singing saloon is now a necessary part of his premises. He is right. Music has its attractions and ever will; but why should it not be rescued from the debasing associations of the public house?

It is necessary to treat with caution such a piece of special pleading, designed to convince his temperance colleagues that comfortable surroundings and good music could be used by them as well as by the publicans. Not all free-and-easies or singing-saloons were as salubrious or as well-run as this. There was a concert room at 34 Trongate in the infamous Tontine Close, feared as a place of robbery, child-stripping and even murder. It is unlikely that they worried whether songs sung there were 'too strong'. Another reviewer criticises the Garrick in Dunlop Street, where the landlord kept a woman for the amusement of the fast men. She 'dresses almost nightly in men's clothes, sings flash, and sometimes indecent songs, and fraternises in a style of the most disgusting familiarity.' For all that, the *Abstainers' Journal* picture of the clientele — well-dressed lads belonging to various handicrafts — accords with such other descriptions as we have.

With regard to theatre attendance we get more detailed information at least for a section of the mid-century audience from reports of the appalling disaster at the Theatre Royal, Dunlop Street, on 17 February 1849. That evening, after the first act of *The Surrender of Calais*, there was an alarm of fire. Smoke was seen coming from the gallery parapet and when a stage carpenter, assisted by two young men from the audience, broke open the panel, flames were seen. The three quickly beat out the flame with their hats and raised a signal cheer. The orchestra began to play. The damage, however, had been done. Though many in the stalls and boxes were unaware that anything untoward had occurred, panic had seized a large number in the gallery at the first sign of fire.

There was a frantic rush to the one exit whose stair led directly to the street. At the ticket-office landing where the stairway turned a few steps above street-level, someone stumbled and fell. Others fell over him, and the blind mob behind crushed forward. When rescuers chopped another exit through the ticket-office to pull people to safety, there were 66 dead or dying victims packed into the small space on the landing.

They were, without exception, working class. The pockets of 66 people revealed 17 shillings and a penny. The majority had no money at all, having saved to raise the threepence for entry to the theatre's cheapest seats. We are reminded of how compact the city was in 1849. These penniless people would have walked home in all directions, to Mile End and Anderston, to Gorbals and Port Dundas. There was none among them from further afield. In terms of class and address we can regard the victims as representative of the gallery audience, estimated at 500.

There are arguments against regarding the ages of the victims as typical. Of the 57 whose ages were recorded, three were under 12 and four over 20; there were 50 between the ages of 12 and 20. Only five of the victims were female, including the two daughters, aged three and 17, of the 42-year-old foreman cork-cutter, Andrew Tonachie, who was also killed. Even if we dismiss the validity of the victims as a sample, on the grounds that the energetic youths might have pushed their way to the stair ahead of the girls and the older people, who may not have panicked, the fact that 50 of the 500 people in the gallery were working-class teenagers is a significant indicator of the importance of theatre-going as a leisure activity for this group.

Not surprisingly, John Henry Alexander — the eccentric, egocentric, exasperating, entertaining 'Alick' — manager at the Theatre Royal, seems to have kept a low profile following the calamity. Some commentators felt it hastened his retirement and death in 1851. In 1850, however, critics were swift to blame his management policy for a slump in attendances, pointing out that when visiting stars appeared the audiences turned out, and complaining that the repertory was too 'heavy'. They drew comparisons with the new 1100-seat house in the fashionable West Nile Street. Prince's Theatre Royal, built by ex-Provost James Lumsden in 1849, quickly became the premier house, with a resident company which included the lessee and manager, Edmund Glover, Miss Fielding, Mrs Ternan, H. F. Lloyd and Sam Cowell. It offered the latest in elegance, comfort and stage design, with a drop scene which cut the visible width of stage from 73 feet to 36, to accommodate the presentation of palace ballroom or humble cot. Sam Bough was scenic artist. For the Christmas show 1849 he painted a panorama of the Royal Fleet in the Clyde, and for an act-drop a view of the Clyde from Dunnottar Hill. Edmund Glover, having made his money from his successful promotion and direction of Jenny Lind's provincial tour in 1848, was convinced of the value of guest artistes. To complement his own experienced cast, whose forte was undoubtedly comedy, during the winter/spring season Glover brought a succession of stars famed for romance or high drama such as Helen Faucit and the Keans; the great MacReady, who had managed the Queen Street Theatre early in the century, came on his farewell provincial tour. Even with these guests, the comedy of Lloyd and Cowell seemed to dominate, though Cowell appeared only in occasional farces and was more frequently employed singing comic songs between pieces. He left the company in May but the summer season, with the eminent comic actor, Mr Ranger, and the Harrison-Pyne Opera Company as guests, was even more frothy. Indeed, in the month of July, of approximately 48 dramatic presentations there were three melodramas and one performance of Home's *Douglas* to show off the talents of the 14-year-old Master Boothby; all the rest was comedy and farce.

The city's third theatre was the Queen's Theatre Royal, built in Greendyke Street on the site of the Adelphi which had burned down in 1848. The proprietor and manager was Mr James Calvert, who had been lessee of the Adelphi. His claim to the 'Theatre Royal' title was dubious since his licence had come from the local magistrates, and that only after an appeal to the Quarter Sessions in November. Calvert was also an experienced manager, having been 24 years at the helm of the Theatre in Abbey Street, Dublin. His highest price was 1s. 6d. He presented a repertory to attract east-end audiences, with an emphasis on 'our national dramas'. Though he did not aspire to the Keans or Miss Faucit, he could on occasion offer a 'popular metropolitan tragedian, Charles Freer, supported by the corps dramatique.'

The Queens was in the prime position to capture audiences during the Glasgow Fair. To obvert this competition Glover leased it himself during the month of July and filled it with a panorama, a Sam Bough diorama, a gymnastic professor and a slack-rope dancer. Just to make sure he added a rope-dancer, Young Hengler, to his own dramatic fare at the Prince's.

Alick responded to the challenge of the new theatres by refurbishing the Theatre Royal and building an extension to the stage accommodation. Calvert seems to have had more influence on his repertory than Glover. He used no big name visitors between reopening in November 1850 and the end of the year, but he leavened his programme with some popular material. In those two months the 60 pieces presented by the company included six Shakespeare plays, eleven Scottish dramas and ten action ballets as well as the Victorian mix of farce and melodrama. The two latter bulk much larger in Glover's programme. He tended to leave the heavy material to the stars, who could draw an audience even to classical tragedy. The remarkable thing is that both managers survived when so many London lessees were going bankrupt.

A night at the theatre demanded stamina but provided value for money, with the curtain at the Prince's rising at 7.30 and coming down at 11.15, if things ran to schedule. In addition to the main production, there would be two or three other items, for instance a short ballet and a farce. Typical prices at Prince's Theatre Royal when there was a visiting star were four shillings for the boxes, three shillings for the stalls and sixpence for the gallery. (A handloom weaver's weekly wage was 6s. 10d.) A 'second price', approximately half, was offered from about nine o'clock. Alexander was an expert in using the two price system. He would run a new spectacular as first piece of the evening for as long as it would pull the crowd; then he would switch it to last place, to draw people at the cheaper rates. In the summer Glover opened at 8.30 and charged only 'second prices' to compete with outdoor attractions.

There was one outdoor drama with which no theatre could compete — the public execution. That of Margaret Lennox Hamilton on 31 January was the first in the city for seven years. Though the press may have differed in their attitudes to the criminal, they were unanimous in deprecating the presentation of the punishment as a public spectacle and were pleased that fewer people attended than previously; a mere 20,000 turned up on a cold, drizzly winter morning! All the papers mention that almost all

113

belonged to the lower classes of society.

It was, of course, Glasgow Green which accommodated these multitudes, and the Green was also the scene of less ghoulish everyday recreations, though they also were governed by class distinctions. Hugh Macdonald, writing in 1854, described how the 'veriest dregs of Glasgow society' gathered at the Saltmarket end to engage in leaping, putting the stone and pitch-and-toss, whereas to the east, in King's Park, the industrious poor spent their weekends playing football, cricket and rounders, or in swimming along at the Dominie's Hole in the Clyde just at Jennie's Burn. Shinty had gone out of fashion, and the 'improvements' had made the sward too smooth and flat for the golf of an earlier era. The football of 1850 had not yet been subdivided into a handling and a dribbling code. Players were allowed to stop the ball with the hand but not to carry it. The sides had been whittled down from the masses of the ritual ball games of village tradition, but the 15 to 20-a-side known in the 1860s to the YMCA lads who formed Queen's Park was probably common. David Murray remembered the students maintaining a kickabout in the College Gardens all day long, with some going off to attend classes while others joined in during a 15-minute break, clad in gown and characteristic high hat.

Football was not a spectator sport. On the Green people would crowd to see rowing matches on the Clyde, either at a regatta week, or in a race for a wager. A hundred enthusiasts gathered for a chess match, though draughts and quoits attracted more betting. Those who recalled a rural childhood might make their way to Govan or Carntyne for a ploughing match. The areas beyond the jurisdiction of the police were also chosen for the larger prize-fights, Mall's Myre being a favourite venue. As mentioned, however, there were a number of the city taverns where a clandestine bout could quickly be set up.

Since pugilism was officially frowned on, boxing booths did not feature at the Fair on Glasgow Green, though fights were not infrequent. For almost 100 years the Fair had started on the second Monday in July, and at midnight on the Sunday prospective stall-holders could be seen lurking in the lanes and closes off Saltmarket ready to dash out with poles and bricks to claim their site in Saltmarket or Trongate. Shows and swings of all kinds extended from the front of the courthouse back on to the Green, and wandering among the booths were the cheapjacks and minor showmen with their halfpenny peepshows. The wonders of science were to be seen in the form of a steam incubator which had already been on show for months at the Argyle Arcade. Wombwell's menagerie was back after a long absence, and carried an added frisson, since his niece had been savaged to death by a tiger earlier that year. Franconi's circus was a little removed from the rest of the shows, in Maxwell

Street, and there was James Cook's permanent circus building in Hope Street. Franconi was also to give several equestrian demonstrations in the College Gardens, open to the public on a commercial basis for the first time, and offering more 'rational' forms of recreation than the shows.

The Green, however, was dominated by the 'Magic Temple' of John Henry Anderson, the Wizard of the North. The previous year he had performed for Queen Victoria at Balmoral. For the whole of 1850 he had billed his show as 'Professor Alexander's Balmoral Entertainment' and now his 200 feet frontage was a 'beautiful representation of Balmoral Castle, Her Majesty's Highland Residence'. It had two compartments each accommodating 1500, one for Anderson's show and one a singing saloon. Sam Sloan, manager of the Odd-Fellows in Saltmarket, was to manage the saloon arrangements, and Sam Cowell was to head the saloon entertainment, assisted by a family of acrobats and a brass band.

In Breckenridge's famous song, 'The Humours of Glasgow Fair', the protagonists rounded off their day by dancing to the fiddle of Blind Alick, one of the famous characters from early in the century. In 1850 a crudely lettered placard outside a Saltmarket cellar still advertised 'Penny Reels' during the Fair. Once the set had taken the floor, the proprietor went round and collected a penny per couple. The fiddler, now the famous McCann instead of Blind Alick, was paid his twopence, struck up the tune and the dancers reeled, set, crossed and cleekit. The Polka Mania had reached the Glasgow stage, and possibly the Trades Hall, but not the Saltmarket cellars.

For those with time to spare, there were leisure activities beyond the city — trips to the coast by train or steamer. It was not unknown for the weekend scrimmage at the Broomielaw to precipitate people into the Clyde. There was less of a crush for the short voyage from the west end of the Green to Rutherglen. The moneyed classes, who might once have gone to Finnieston or Kilpatrick for the goat-whey season, would now take a house at the coast for a month, with the breadwinner coming down at weekends.

Changes in leisure activity would come in time. Stricter licensing from 1854 limited the number of spirit shops. By the end of the fifties the council had acquired two parks and an art gallery. Organised football, and ultimately commercial spectator sport, began with Queen's Park Football Club in 1867. Shorter working hours meant that entertainments could start and finish earlier. Custom-built music halls developed alongside the singing saloons. Until the 20th century, however, entertainment remained, as it was in 1850, communal and live.

Æt. XCll.

'Senex' — Robert Reid (1773-1865)

116

THEY WROTE ABOUT GLASGOW: A TRIBUTE

CHARLES A. OAKLEY

I was 16 years old when I came to Glasgow to serve a six-year apprenticeship as a naval architect in John Brown's shipyard. The First World War was in its penultimate year. My father had been a member of the management team at Devonport Dockyard. He had died in his mid-40s, a consequence of a mischance while bringing a warship, damaged in a collision off Portland Point, into the Dockyard.

He had wanted me to follow him into shipbuilding, but into a private yard. The thinking was that, after the war was over, there would be virtually no call for warships, but an almost insatiable demand for new mercantile ships to replace the hundreds torpedoed during the hostilities.

I had fallen in with this idea somewhat reluctantly. My headmaster had suggested accounting for me, because mathematics was my best subject or journalism (because of the articles and drawings I contributed to the school magazine).

During his long illness my father had been visited by colleagues who had been seconded as overseers to the northern shipyards to ensure that the Admiralty's requirements were strictly observed. They favoured my father's ideas about my future and all agreed that Glasgow was preferable to Liverpool or Newcastle. 'Living was best there,' they said.

It was the Second City of the Empire. Lights were brighter then. Entertainments flourished on Clydeside: Glasgow had several good theatres, music halls, as well as 100 cinemas.

When I reached Clydebank I was in for a humbling surprise. I was to start as the 'boy' in the 'safe', where plans in current use were kept. I was very kindly treated — I must have been raw. My soft Cornish accent (which is akin to Welsh) was mistaken for Irish and when, in the passing of time, it had been overlapped by some 'Glesca', the blend came out very like Northern Irish. This explains why I am still mistaken for an Ulsterman, particularly throughout Ireland itself.

My greatest regret was in having no close friends. I lived in Hyndland, where the Admiralty headquarters was located, and so left Clydebank every afternoon about five o'clock. I remained a bit of a loner, until in the autumn of 1919 I entered Glasgow University.

Actually, I had had a startling experience on my very first Saturday evening in the city. I had come out of a cinema about seven o'clock and was swept along in a crowd rushing to something highly spectacular going on in George

117

Square. Here, next to the Head Post Office, a very tall warehouse was going up in stupendous flames. Glasgow certainly did things in a big way.

My earliest disappointment with the people of Glasgow was that they could tell me so little about their city. I asked them questions about something that had interested me and the usual answer was 'I don't know', with the implication 'I don't care either'. I told several that I heard there was a very fine square called Blythswood, near Sauchiehall Street, but, astonishing as it might now seem, weeks passed before I found my own way there. And the yarns told me about this place called Dixon's Blazes now seem unbelievable.

Forty years later, in 1962, I was given the privilege of writing the book *The Last Tram*, when the city's tramway system was being closed down. I accepted with warm enthusiasm because I had found my way round Glasgow largely by tram car. At first this was done just on Saturday afternoons, going to football matches.

Shortly after arriving at Clydebank to begin my apprenticeship I noticed that one of Glasgow's football clubs was called Partick Thistle. On going each working day from Hyndland to Clydebank I had first to go down to Partick to board a tram or a train. One of the journeymen explained Thistle's ground was not in Partick at all but in Maryhill. Inevitably I lost my way. Eventually, by heading towards the roars of approval and dissent, I got there in time to go in by the boys' half-time gate.

The next week I felt confident I could make my way by Green Tram to the East End (I had never been there before). Rangers were to play Celtic. My fellow apprentices warned me that there would be noisy, rough crowds, but I had not expected to be compressed and shoved about in such a throng. Suddenly bedlam was let loose. 'Fister' Walls laid out Patsy Gallagher with a most vicious kick on the shin. There was uproar around me, the Rangers supporters insisting that Patsy must have said something very offensive to Fister. A stretcher appeared on the field but Patsy was able to walk off. I felt that if he had got on the stretcher murder would have taken place in my vicinity. Patsy was a joiner in John Brown's. When it became known that I had actually witnessed the outrage I was pressed for comment on the Rangers' assertions about Patsy having started the trouble. I just didn't know about that but said I was going to support Queen's Park. From then on my fellow apprentices took a pretty poor view of such pusillanimity. But it did have one particular advantage for me in that I now found myself in a quite splendid part of the City of Glasgow. I had never seen the like of it before. Indeed, I even found my first girlfriend there. The white trams had brought me to her.

ON TO THE MITCHELL

In 1919 when I matriculated at the University I rejoiced in being in such a different environment. No need to keep a lookout for testy, bowler-hatted foremen. Among the discoveries I made while in the Students' Union was a method of earning welcome pocket money. This was by dabbling in freelance journalism.

Glasgow in those enlightened days had three evening newspapers: *Evening Times, Evening News* and *Evening Citizen.* I began sending in short articles (600 words) on what were regarded as topical subjects (with a Glasgow flavour). The articles had, of course, to be typed, even if the author had to do the job himself, using two fingers, or, indeed, even one, with the other sometimes daringly darting in.

I tried my hand at this lark and did better than most (some critics might comment that I have never stopped). What really helped was my interest in odd and unusual things I came across here and there in Glasgow and my persistence in asking questions about them. (Dare I say, in passing, that I got some of my best finds in the Necropolis and from some decidedly strange strangers I came across.)

But the really big moment in my career came when I found my way into the Mitchell Library's Glasgow Room. It was situated on the ground floor adjacent to the Main Reading Hall. It had never occurred to my friends (particularly the girls) to pop their heads inside to see what was going on. When I took the risk I was quite astounded.

There were shelves and shelves of books about Glasgow, standing upright and bristling with the challenge to read them. Ever since I arrived in Glasgow I had been belly-aching about the city not having books such as I had read as a boy about Plymouth, with its maritime history, its barbican and its riviera hinterland.

Why on earth had I not been told about these Glasgow books? Well, when I began to look at them I discovered that most had actually been written in the 1800s. That was when Glaswegians really had deep-seated convictions about the greatness of their city. We know little about John McUre who wrote about Glasgow quite early in the 1700s. John Gibson penned a very useful account later in the century of the rise of the Tobacco Lords. (And what a lot they turned out to have been.) The first of Glasgow's outstanding historians was unquestionably Robert Reid, who used the pseudonym 'Senex' (and is still best remembered by that title). He thought himself the greatest of them all — and, in fact, he was. A long-time member of the Chamber of Commerce he was immersed in the business world — he had actually served his apprenticeship in one of David Dale's cotton weaving mills. He was a prolific author and his many articles and other papers were gathered together and indexed by two other prominent writers, Dr Mathie Hamilton and John Buchanan. And then, in 1884, these were revised with an additional section, written by John Carrick, and one of the most detailed indexes I have ever seen. They are bound in three volumes.

There were others too, such as James Pagan, editor of the *Glasgow Herald*, who took occasional Sunday afternoon walks round the place and wrote about the city's amazing expansion. And again, there was James Cleland, the brilliant town planner, who laid out the centre of the city along straight lines from Glasgow Cross to Charing Cross and into the West End. Rightly he has his portrait in the City Chambers. Central Glasgow is a model of what the centre of a major city should look like. Manchester is not in the same class, Liverpool even less and Birmingham a disaster.

Next on my list is Peter Mackenzie, a journalist with a leaning to the left. Then there is Dr John Strang, the City Chamberlain, who prepared a detailed account of Glasgow's rise to be the Empire's Second City. John Tweed compiled biographies of every Lord Provost from 1833 to 1883. They clearly were all strong-willed men and perhaps not all that easy to deal with.

In some respects that might be said of J. O. Mitchell himself. He was the outstanding figure in the last years of the Victorian age and carried on into the new era. He was a prosperous businessman engaged in the leather trade — some might have described him as a bit snobbish because he followed his account of *One Hundred Glasgow Men* with a rather ostentatious description of *Old Country Houses of the Old Glasgow Gentry*.

Two late Victorian authors whose works lingered on into the early Edwardian years were Dr Robert Renwick whose *Glasgow Memorials* was the first part of the city's official history. Another well-known Glasgow figure, George Eyre-Todd, wrote the third volume. So little interest was shown by 20th century readers that the Corporation allowed the series to lapse.

These memorials and companion works made heavy reading, as I discovered in my student days when going through them looking for stories quaint and amusing. But allowing for Victorian verbosity they are very well put together — and certainly contain unexpected information on diverting and interesting happenings in the comparatively recent past.

This is a point at which I must make an admission. I too am a Victorian; that is to say, I was born while Queen Victoria was still on her throne. I was actually at her funeral. She died in 1901 at Osborne House on the Isle of Wight in the arms of the Kaiser, her favourite grandson. (You are not often told that.) Her coffin was brought to Portsmouth where the funeral ceremonies began in the Dockyard Church, before the coffin was conveyed by train (covered by black drapings) to London and thence to St Paul's. No, I was not just among the crowds outside. I was at the ceremony, but, as I was just a few months old and slept peacefully through it all, I have no recollection of the great occasion.

I must admit that, if there had been one period in which I would have most liked living in Glasgow, it is the Edwardian, from the end of the Boer War up to the time when people first sensed that the Roaring Twenties were over, with the Wall Street Crash in the offing.

The new century had seen two splendid exhibitions staged at Kelvingrove and the business world had been considerably impressed. No matter what manufactured product was mentioned you would be told of at least one company in Greater Glasgow that could provide it and, needless to say, of the finest quality. Almost unbelievable as it seemed there were no fewer than 22 shipyards on the Clyde and they were launching nearly half of all the ships in the world. No wonder Grand Duke Alexis of Russia when on a visit had said that Glasgow must be 'the centre of the intelligence in England'. But the new century was to bring about great change in the kind of books being produced in the city. The Victorians had written exclusively for themselves. They liked their books — even their stories — that way. Quite a different work was published in 1901 and it immediately won great praise as 'the best book about Glasgow seen for a very long time'. *Glasgow in 1901* was something new.

It saw splendid things ahead. The author was given as J. H. Muir, but that was just a pseudonym for three very young people. They were James Bone, who was to become one of Fleet Street's most influential editors, Archie Charteris, who rose to be one of Australia's leading lawyers, and Muirhead Bone, the brilliant artist who settled down as one of Oxford's favourite dwellers — all this within a comparatively brief time of his forecasting a brilliant future for their native city.

As in so many other areas, the First World War proved to be a watershed in writing about Glasgow. Those authors who survived it (and the Second War, too) are radically different from their predecessors. I am inclined to mention as my favourite, Neil Munro's *The Brave Days*. The writer came to the city as a youngish lad, revelled in Glasgow's life and rose to become one of its most esteemed newspaper editors. He certainly knew his way around.

I never met him but I had close associations with John Buchan, certainly the most widely known of the city's authors of that period. Indeed, he ended his career as Governor General of Canada, and that is pretty high up. We were associated through the cinema, first in the formation, when he was one of the Scottish Universities' three MPs, of the British Film Institute in London in the early 1930s, and then the Scottish Film Council, of which he was the first Chairman (and I succeeded him). His autobiography *Memory Hold the Door* includes a quite captivating account of his student days in the 1890s at Glasgow University.

O. H. Mavor (James Bridie) is a product of student life after the turn of the century. He and his friend Walter Elliot early achieved notability in the city. On his return after the war he turned to the theatre and, along with a new crony, J. B. Priestley, became the outstanding playwright of 1935-50.

In my early student days in the 1920s I came very much under his influence — indeed, I was regarded as one of his protégés (we were both better known as cartoonists before descending to writing). And when in the middle of the Second World War he founded the Citizens' Theatre, I was associated with the venture and am now Hon. President. But we were never close. For one thing, he thought it a piece of impudence for me to attempt to write *The Second City*.

However, he was also lacking in enthusiasm for Dr A. J. Cronin's *Dr Finlay's Casebook*. And here I must switch to Mavor's cousin, Guy McCrone (actually he was a late Victorian, whereas Mavor was Edwardian). McCrone's *Wax Fruit* (*Red Plush* in the United States) was fantastically successful and was translated into several foreign languages. It delineated life in one of Glasgow's wealthy business circles and many of the leading characters, I was assured, could be readily identified.

For some reason I have a great liking for Frederick Niven's *The Staff at Simpson's*. And I would like to slip in a note of appreciation for James Cowan (Peter Prowler) and his *From Glasgow's Treasure Chest*. Employed in a city warehouse he spent many of his lunch breaks seeking out bits of information about the forgotten past. His book is quite fascinating. And I certainly cannot leave out two men who created Glasgow characters who became known throughout Britain, J. J. Bell (Wee Macgreegor) and R. W. Campbell (Spud Tamson).

At the beginning of the Second World War I was one of Glasgow University's staff nominated for secondment to the Civil Service. I soon found myself in the Air Ministry and then Scottish Controller of the Ministry of Aircraft Production, and in the later stages of the war (believe it or not) Controller for the North of Ireland too. I had 100,000 workpeople in my Scottish coterie and another 40,000 in Ireland. As if this was not variegated enough I was told that I was to be switched at the end of the war to be Scottish Controller of the Board of Trade. However, there was to be a gap of about six weeks in between and a good way occurred to me in which I could spend this time. As I would need that book about Glasgow I had always been looking for since I crossed the border 30 years before and as no-one seemed disposed to write it, I decided to have a shot at it myself. And I would begin with all those old volumes in the Mitchell Library's Glasgow Room.

I spent several hours there every day, though it might be remarked that I had not done much actual research. I had read my way through up to 20 of the Victorian books and had selected the material for my book from them. And, although photography was virtually unknown in many of the Victorian years, many very able black and white artists had been busy in the streets and skilled craftsmen had prepared blocks to facilitate their reproduction in magazines.

The second half of the book presented me with fewer problems than the first. Not only had I been writing for the press since the early 1920s but, after my return to the city in 1930, I had been contributing articles galore to the Chamber of Commerce monthly *Journal*. Indeed, after a few years I had virtually taken over much of the editorship and had made wide use of the city's splendid press photographers. Most of the illustrations covering the last half century came from them, partly for reproduction in the *Journal*, partly by private commissions. I am very grateful to them. In all we now have in the book no fewer than three hundred pictures.

When, after my six weeks of very hard slog, towards the end of 1946 it became clear that I had indeed achieved my purpose, I then discussed the project with the city's two leading book publishers, Blackie and Collins. Both were willing to take the book on, and as Blackie were willing to go right ahead, I signed up with them.

The book was an astonishing success. Clearly the Glasgow public had wanted it. After three printings, each of 5000 copies, sales settled down and have never ceased. The fact that it is thoroughly indexed no doubt helps. I have no use for books of this kind if they are perfunctorily indexed, or, worse, not indexed at all.

The Second City has at the time of Glasgow's year as Europe's Culture Capital undergone another revision, bringing it up to date. In all it has seven fresh editions and reprintings. In fact, the 1990 edition seems to have remarkably little resemblance to the first, 1940, edition.

MODEL YACHT POND AND CLUB HOUSE CAMPHILL PARK, GLASGOW.

E 02914

Queen's Park c.1915

DEAR GREEN PLACE: Recollections of Glasgow Parks

CORDELIA OLIVER

LONG BEFORE I knew that the name of my native city, Glasgow, might possibly derive from the phrase, 'dear green place', I had discovered for myself the essential truth of that description as it related to my own surroundings. Not that I grew up in specially privileged circumstances, with a lush garden to play in: I was born in a flat in a quiet, respectable street on the south side, now bulldozed to make way for the Kingston motorway. The Pollok Street of my infancy was a genteel, early 19th century avenue with plain Georgian frontages and a central, railed-in garden planted with mature, shady trees — limes, I suppose — in which a variety of birds nested, sang and chattered endlessly. The dawn chorus must have wakened many who slept in the 'best' front bedrooms.

Behind our first floor flat with its Greek Key plasterwork and polished brass door furniture, was a cultivated back green with flower beds and bushes of lilac and laburnum. An immensely tall ash tree against the back wall towered above everything, frustrating all juvenile attempts to grow even nasturtiums around its hefty roots. That same ash tree was the stuff of family legend: before my time there was a parrot that escaped through the kitchen window one summer morning to perch on a branch far out of reach so that firemen had to be called to the rescue. The parrot survived to die of old age and, indeed, to live on, stuffed, under a bell glass on the kitchen dresser from where he fixed us all with a disconcertingly beady eye. Joey was the parrot's name, and I think he disappeared during our removal to Pollokshields.

Maxwell Park was the first real paradise of my childhood; the place where, in pre-school summers, under watchful grown-up eyes, I learned to make my first clumsy daisy chains and to suck the 'honey' from clover flowers (no worries, then, about catching deadly diseases from friendly doggies). And by the time I could read *Peter Pan in Kensington Gardens* for myself I was already translating Barrie's London fantasy land into Maxwell Park. Our little pond in Pollokshields became the Serpentine, and hardly any imagination was needed to see weird Arthur Rackham creatures in the Maxwell Park trees. Only a few years later one would be memorising Latin numerals by repetition — unus . . . duo . . . tres — as one thrust oneself higher and higher on a swing. Yes, Maxwell Park was (and it still is) the perfect playground, with its wide meadow for ball games, its safe, shallow pond for toy sailing boats (once, there were swans with their cygnets, but no longer, alas) and its shrubberies for hide-and-seek — an endless source of adventure until, grown to teenage maturity one discovered that the whole, wonderful paradise covers an astonishingly small acreage between the railway and the villas in St Andrew's Drive.

Pollok Estate was different: then, as now, it was a remarkable pocket of *rus in urbe*. Pollok, with its bluebell wood in which, at the age, even, of 11 or 12, one could enjoy the thrill of feeling far away from everyone. Pollok was special, a real paradise, with its grassy rides and its lake where 'baggie minnies' obligingly swam straight into jamjars (back at home the poor little frogs that materialised were fated to be released on to the grass, doubtless to die unhappy and disoriented) and waterfowl chucked and quacked as they dived for sustenance.

Who cared, at that age, that this amazing stretch of what seemed like 'real' country within the boundary of a large industrial city didn't just happen of its own accord but was actually the creation of an unusually caring and forward-looking landowner. Sir John Stirling Maxwell, who inherited Pollok on coming of age in 1888, not only created the gardens and, indeed, the landscape as we know it today, but was what we now call amenity conscious long before the fashion developed. Aware of his duty to the community, he made a large part of the park available to the public and allowed the edges to be nibbled by playing fields. The fact that, after his death, Sir John's daughter made a gift to the city of the whole estate now seems like no more than a continuation of her father's magnanimity. Sir John could not possibly have foreseen that this gift would open the way to the housing of the Burrell Collection in its now world-famous gallery at Pollok, but there is little doubt that such a happy consummation would have given him great satisfaction.

The Burrell Gallery, with its imaginative siting to give wonderful close-up woodland vistas through its great glass windows, offers new opportunities to experience the magical seasonal changes from the warm, dry comfort of indoors, but childhood memories of Glasgow's parks seem inseparable from summer sunshine. Ringwood, however, was different; not really a park but a hillside reached by climbing over a stile at the top of Springkell Avenue. Cows grazed there; the local riding school would be met on the bridle path, and that was where in spring we rolled our easter eggs, and went tobogganing on the rare winter snow. Ringwood is now an estate of would-be grand, modern houses, each squeezed into an insignificant plot of ground.

Parks farther away from home were visited in adult company; some on a regular basis; others more seldom, and for specific reasons. Rouken Glen, for example, was a frequent tram ride on summer Saturdays, just far enough away to count as an excursion. Rouken Glen was another, earlier, gift from a beneficent landowner (Cameron Corbett, later Lord Rowallan, presented the estate to Glasgow in 1903) and a visit offered what seemed like an endless choice of experiences and activities. One could walk through the glen, verdurous and shady, to see the waterfall once described by Christopher North as 'one of the loneliest and loveliest linns that ever sounded in the solitary silence of nature'. Or, if one's luck were in, there might be trips in a rowing boat round the leafy islands in the lake, and later, maybe, there would be ice-cream in the tearoom. Boating at Rouken Glen was to become part of one's romantic adolescence, but that comes outwith the scope of this essay.

The tram ride itself is remembered as an adventure, especially when fortune smiled and one of the old, open-ended cars rattled along to the tram stop at the right time. One of Ian Hamilton Finlay's poems from 'Glasgow Beasts' puts it in a nutshell:

anither
time
ah wis a
minnie
aw
the pond
haw
the shoogly caur . . .

Rouken Glen, no longer a Glasgow park since its hiving off to the care of Eastwood District, is still there and thriving as a pleasure ground with its lake and its glen and its waterfall, its garden centre and its great new excitement for youngsters and adults alike — the now famous Butterfly Farm. Buses long ago replaced the 'shoogly caurs' of my own and Ian Finlay's youth, but the outing surely holds as much enjoyment today as it did in the 1930s.

Tollcross Park was visited seldom by comparison, simply because, as a park, it had less to offer and, no doubt, because, lying to the east of the city, it seemed that much farther away. But Tollcross Park had one unique, unrivalled attraction. Like most of the city parks it centred on a former mansion house and in that house was a children's museum which contained the main reason for the visit. This was a taxidermist's set piece in a big glass case: 'Who killed Cock Robin? I said the Sparrow, with My Bow and Arrow. Who saw him die? I, said the Fly, with my little Eye. . . .' all the 'players' were present to be searched for among the foliage. Would any six-year-old, in this age of fabulous wild-life camerawork on television, till feel a comparable sense of anticipation at setting out across the city to renew acquaintanceship with a case of stuffed birds and insects, no matter how cleverly set out to illustrate a familiar nursery rhyme? I doubt it very much.

Queen's Park was much nearer home and that, too, was a regular jaunt for summer Saturdays, not least when the model yacht club went into action. Electronic remote control was then unknown: the boats in question were real scale model yachts with sails and rigging and masts as tall as a man. With the unthinking childish relish of disaster one always hoped to see a vessel capsize, but none ever did in my experience.

Queen's Park, with its Roman campsite, was, of course, 'educational', although little of what one was told at the time was seriously listened to, except for the fact that the queen in question (queens were always more romantic than Roman soldiers) was Mary, Queen of Scots and not Queen Victoria who seemed to have lent her name to almost everything else including, of course, Victoria Road, which leads to the park's impressive main gates. Queen's Park is actually rather splendid with its Paxton stairway and terrace and its fine views from the flagstaff at Camphill. But somehow it is the memory of the pond and the big sailing ships that overshadows everything else.

Victoria Park, over in Partick, offered another excuse for an occasional Saturday sortie. The Fossil Grove — Glasgow's own 'petrified forest' — cannot have altered much since the early 1930s when I first went there with my grandmother. The fossils in question were formed from the roots and stumps of trees that grew there some 200 million years ago, an almost unimaginable infinity in those more innocent days but perhaps less impressive in the world of today when everyone seems to speak of 'billions', and a mere million seems small beer.

For years Bellahouston Park was no more to me than a pair of gateposts at the end of Nithsdale Road. Quite simply, with Maxwell Park and Pollok so much nearer home, there was nothing at Bellahouston to make a special excursion worthwhile. But in 1938, with the Empire Exhibition, this park came to life in a spectacular fashion. Here, as with Queen's Park, the land rises to an eminence giving a wide view all around, and much was made of this in the design of the Exhibition, with Tait's Tower crowning the hilltop. Now there's nothing left of that memorable extravaganza but the memory of the snow-white Art Deco pavilions and the wide avenues and staircases with their waterspouts and fountains (the funfair, of course, was a summer-long attraction, presaging the recent Garden Festival) and it is ironic that the one structure designed for permanence, the so-called Palace of Art, should also be the dullest in design.

Now, of course, there's an artificial ski-slope for the energetic, and a building based on Charles Rennie Mackintosh's 'House for an Art Lover' is to be a permanent feature in the Park. But since the drawings on which this reconstruction is based, famous as they are from repeated reproduction, were never more than a first set of plans and elevations for a competition run by a German magazine, and since nobody can possibly tell what crucial alterations Mackintosh, essentially a 'site architect' (a spatial sculptor, you might say), would have made if actually commissioned to build the house, this is, to say the least, a doubtful exercise. Within a space of 20 years, even, will visitors to Bellahouston Park look on the building as a genuine work by Mackintosh?

Glasgow's real dividing line is not drawn between east and west or north and south, but between West End and South Side. For someone brought up, as I was, in Pollokshields, the West End seemed almost as far away as Edinburgh. Almost, but not quite, since there were relatives to be visited across the river, usually on Sunday afternoons, and it was then that one would be taken to Kelvingrove or to the Botanic Gardens. Walking along the banks of the Kelvin one would listen to tales of the great exhibitions the park had housed around the turn of the century, exhibitions full of exotic buildings of which the Art Galleries are a permanent reminder, the over-elaborate structure built for the 1901 International Exhibition with the profits of the previous one in 1888. It is often asked why Glasgow's Art Gallery boasts two main entrances and why the 'back door' is even grander than the *porte-cochère* on Argyle Street. The reason is, of course, that the building was designed to face the park during the 1901 Exhibition, but afterwards to face the main thoroughfare from which most of its visitors would enter.

Kelvingrove Park, like Queen's Park, bears the touch of Sir Joseph Paxton who added his own magic to an already dramatic landscape. To look up at the University, that grandiose Folly on Gilmorehill, or at Park Terrace with its flagstaff and the attendant guns which were captured at Sebastopol, is actually more impressive than looking down from above. There were gondolas on the Kelvin in 1911 and the tale is still told of a town councillor's gaffe at the meeting where the proposal was made to put a Venetian gondola on the river during the Exhibition. 'Why not bring a pair' said the gentleman in question, 'and let them breed'.

A visit to Glasgow's Botanic (*not* Botanical) Gardens inevitably meant a walk through the Kibble Palace, and how vast it seemed, that soaring glass structure with its tropical tree ferns reflected in the water. The comforting warmth, too, on a winter afternoon (for some reason I think of the Kibble Palace as part of a Christmas holiday outing) is never to be forgotten. Even then I knew that this impressively grand glasshouse with its huge, circular dome had once been in a private garden somewhere down the Clyde (in fact it was at Coulport on Loch Long) and had been taken to pieces and brought to Kelvinside late last century. What I didn't know until much later, when I married a keen photographer and local historian, was that the same wealthy magnate, John Kibble, who had commissioned the palace of glass (could it possibly have been designed by the ubiquitous 'Crystal Palace' Joseph Paxton?) had also designed a camera so massive that it had to be moved by horse power.

During his time as Director of Glasgow Art Galleries and Museums, Dr Tom Honeyman found himself confronting the problem of what to do with the army of Victorian marble statuary which then populated the central hall at Kelvingrove. His solution was to place some of them among the greenery in the Kibble Palace, and there they remain to most people's satisfaction, sculpture and vegetation being natural companions.

I have always felt blessed by fortune in being brought up by a grandmother, with a resident great-aunt, both of whom retained a keen interest in Glasgow history and legend. Glasgow Green was part of that education; the old town common, and possibly the oldest official 'public park' in the UK. By any standard the Green is a remarkable survival in the heart of a huge industrial city; a real common people's pleasure ground by the riverside, richly wooded and spacious as a Duke's estate. More exciting, however, and decidedly more awe-inspiring, were the occasions when we climbed up through the Necropolis, higher and higher among the exotic tombs until we could look down on the spire of the Cathedral and the great warehouses of what is now known as the 'merchant city', with John Knox looming over us from the top of a column that seemed to bulge outward under his weight. A few years ago I took the Romanian artist Paul Neagu up into the Necropolis on a day of mists that made it seem like the perfect setting for one of Webster's tragedies. Neagu, looking positively vampirish in his black Transylvanian cloak and hat, declared that he found this multi-faceted celebration of Death as fascinating as anything else in Glasgow.

THE MAKING OF A MOTORING HISTORIAN

GEORGE A. OLIVER

I BEGAN to be a motoring historian in the Mitchell Library in Glasgow some time in 1936 by taking out two volumes of *The Autocar* for 1914 and making from them a number of small pencil drawings of contemporary cars. I have them still, the paper wizened now, but the quality of the drawings still perceptible. They showed no particular preference; I was trying my hand; exploring; sampling what was available in a year of particular automobile significance — and finding out in the passing what it was that made men laugh then when the subject of old cars came up.

The sheer improbability of so much on wheels — whether two, three or four — had occurred to me often. It had not crossed my mind, however, that it had been going on since the practical beginnings of the motor-car in the mid 80s and that a good deal more had happened since 1914. In time I was to live among those odd objects that occupy the automobile engineers' heaven.

In 1936 I was 16 years old. Young as I was my qualifications were already high and had credentials been required for what was, after all, a self-appointed task I could have produced them by the score. It was a matter of observation; observation the whole year round, morning and night, winter and summer and the bits in between, with no let up. All traffic that moved within my vicinity was noted — I missed nothing, not even those odd-looking Garrett 'ghost trains' that once carried our city's rubbish. But it was still only one of many interests at that time and as far as I know I managed to grow up in a reasonably normal way.

Already, before I went near the Mitchell, I had a pretty wide knowledge of such periodicals as *The Autocar, The Motor, The Light Car, The Motor World, Automobile Engineering* and *Commercial Motor*. My knowledge of motoring literature, past and present, was much above the average so that by all normal standards I was well equipped. In actual fact I knew little about most makes of car and tackling *The Autocar*, literally and pictorially, as a source of motoring history was one way of remedying this situation. Or so it seemed to one who hoped to earn his living before long as an automobile artist and writer.

By then I did know a little about drawing commercial vehicle chassis and coachwork; I had been working from Albion and Thornycroft plans; makes with which my father had been associated. And towards the late 1930s I began to draw cars as well. Thereafter I drew cars to all intents and purposes as anatomical specimens, using them as objects of detailed study. Then my

Scottish Motor Show in Kelvin Hall 1931 from *Municipal Undertakings* 1932

drawings were tiny — a matter of two or three inches across, as a rule — and although I gradually developed a slightly larger style that would stretch to the width of a magazine page on occasion, basically I was a small-scale worker. That changed drastically at the end of the 60s when I made my first book. Then, I had to produce measured drawings of old cars at one-eighth actual size and had to find a way of doing this convincingly in line.

Unlike most small boys who were always very much more concerned in next year's cars than this I had a more-than-passing interest in vehicles of earlier times and between 1936 and 1939 I was forever in the Mitchell, learning a great deal about their form from the pages of *The Autocar*. Its readers were generously treated, with good text, photographs and drawings in great profusion, and coverage on an international scale. One object of that first visit to the Mitchell was to see how my new drawings compared with recent ones made from surviving old cars in Kelvingrove Art Gallery. I found that it was possible to make a very reasonable translation into pencil, from photographs up to about six inches wide. To begin with the notes I made were brief and it was not until much later that I began to expand them. I still looked upon myself largely as an automobile illustrator.

But already I had taken on an additional literary responsibility — though it was not to be more fully developed until very much later. I had, I felt, a responsibility towards the history of the motor-vehicle that had to be expressed in some literary and pictorial form eventually — but when and how was beyond my comprehension then. I knew, in a vague sort of way, that I had to respond eventually; and that was all. There was nothing especially patriotic about this; by then Albion was the sole survivor of the Scottish motor industry and while I retained an interest in the make I knew little or nothing about the rest of the cars once made here.

At intervals I went back to the Mitchell to continue with my studies of *The Autocar* and from 1937 onwards I was a full-time student at Glasgow School of Art. From 1938 I was so bored by life-drawing that I took to the streets with my sketchbook and concentrated on drawing buildings, motor-vehicles and ships. That was when I also began to make finished drawings of modern cars, in line.

Between 1940 and 1946 I was in the Air Force and finished up in India where there were many elderly motor-vehicles. There, too, there were no petty restrictions and I could draw wherever I pleased. The latest shapes of American cars were something of an eye-opener; our own cars I knew well but it was interesting to get up to date with the makes of other countries, seen here in some cases for the first time.

When I returned to Scotland I was a much better equipped motoring historian on the pictorial side but what I had to catch up on then was the written word. Although I was back at the Art School I still spent a fair amount of time in the Mitchell pursuing a project for my Diploma that involved some pages of a projected pictorial and written history of the motor-car. My idea was to have a continuous strip throughout the book, with colour silhouettes of cars, from the very earliest, placed in front of line drawings of buildings. At intervals in the text there would be larger drawings of cars of especial importance. All the illustrations were in profile and drawn very accurately. The narrative was to be terse but also accurate.

When I came back to Glasgow in 1946 I had a new interest. I was now reasonably well acquainted with the history of the three leading Scottish makes of car — Albion, Argyll and Arrol-Johnston (Albion until 1913, that is) — and was keen to learn more about others. That year there were 50th anniversary celebrations of various kinds and some surviving cars of Scottish make made public appearances. In 1949 I got to know John Sword who, at that time, was collecting old cars the way I was collecting books on motoring, and he was extremely generous, giving me the run of a Collection that by 1950 already numbered more than 100.

In my schooldays one of the boys' papers ran a series about a youngster who was able to go back in time whenever he pleased, so that taking part in the battle of Agincourt, or Waterloo, for example, was no problem. I now found myself with the same kind of facility, with the difference that I could step back into any period of motoring history in one or other of the sheds that housed the Sword Collection.

It was round about the same time that I also got to know some of the more senior men who had had close links with the Scottish car industry, including George Cutbush, who had been editor of *The Motor World* for more than 40 years, and A. K. Stevenson who was then Secretary of the Royal Scottish Automobile Club. Very gradually I began to build up a bank of material and knowledge, but it was never easy.

For a number of years I found other things to do and it was 1958 before my first real chance came along. I was asked to write and illustrate a book on early cars and as it happened I was living temporarily beside the Sword Collection. So I chose to draw twelve of the cars at Balgray, in Ayrshire, where the Collection was housed, and to write about them in extended captions. For a great deal of my text and caption material I had to refer repeatedly to *The Autocar* and I began to fill notebooks as well as sketchbooks. I discovered a latent ability as a writer of captions and as a recaller of times past. This I began to develop increasingly. My earliest memory of a motor vehicle probably went back to 1923, after all.

Living with the Sword Collection for a couple of years and being associated with it for much longer had been an enormous asset. It gave me instant access to the past, with a great variety of makes from most car-producing nations instantly available. In that first book I chose to draw cars of four different nations, Britain, America, France and Germany. Subsequently I was able to bring in cars of Italian make as well, which enlarged the scope of my books quite considerably. Marketing was important even then in the limited editions I was responsible for.

Over several years I made four of these records of motor-cars built between 1896 and 1930 as well as a History of the Racing Car. In between times I wrote the story of the Rover Car Company and a History of Coachbuilding. Then, in 1980, I was commissioned to write an illustrated history of the British motor industry: the idea which had been simmering since 1936 was at last realised. Again I used the Mitchell Library, now with a much fuller understanding: to *The Autocar* I owe a great deal not simply in terms of information but as a direct influence for good on my writing.

A few years later, around 1986, I began to think again, more seriously than ever, about the Scottish industry and about making a proper record of it even although I knew that there was little chance of having such a book published at that time. I took it on as a long term project and began to study Company history, at leisure, in the Records Office in Edinburgh. In many instances this was a revelation, business methods varying greatly, particularly in the early years. Later — inevitably — I returned to the Mitchell to intensify my research in the files of magazines. One discovery I made there was that the publication, *Motor Traction*, had a Scot on its staff before the First World War and that he had fed it with a succession of good stories.

About one quarter of the cars, lorries and buses made in Scotland came from the Glasgow area but it is as difficult to find out about them here as anywhere else. Mostly the factories have disappeared; indeed only the former Albion plant at Scotstoun survives still, and while the Argyll factory remains at Alexandria, there is less to see every time one passes it. Until 1914 the Scottish car makers, Albion, Argyll and Arrol-Johnston did very well in terms of publicity in the motoring press, and this attention continued even after 1914, when Argyll went out of business. This was not a matter of output for between 1909 and 1914 Argyll production at no time exceeded 622 yet numerous references were made to the make in the motoring press throughout this period, Alex Govan, the Managing Director of Argyll until his premature death in 1907, was an excellent publicist and obviously passed on his skill. Edinburgh's one-and-only City Astronomer, Sir William Peck, was also good at promoting not only his own subject but also the self-propelled vehicles he seemed to spend all his spare time designing.

These days, I spend all my spare time in writing a history of the industry in Scotland, with about 80 cars, lorries and buses to deal with. Once I might have claimed that it would be definitive. Older and far wiser I now make no such claim: too much has disappeared for ever.

THE MISERIES OF HOPE:
JAMES MACFARLAN (1832-1862)

HAMISH WHYTE

The story is told of how the Glasgow pedlar-poet James Macfarlan on his travels one September day had walked 15 miles of country road when night came down. He hoped to reach the house of a friend five miles ahead, but did not have the strength to continue. He stopped at a farm to ask for lodging. The farmer set a dog on him and he had to spend the night in the fields with cold turnips for supper. That in essence is the story of Macfarlan's life: door after door, literal and figurative, shut in his face. Confirmed in his anguish as a poet of genius battering at the gates of Fame, he never broke through, and died of consumption in squalor in a Drygate attic on 6 November 1862, aged 30.

Other contemporaries of comparable talent and circumstances, such as Alexander Smith, James Thomson, David Gray and Robert Buchanan, achieved some measure of fame and, if not fortune, comfort. Why not Macfarlan? The short answer is his lack of stability. He was shiftless, a wanderer by nature. He was his own worst enemy. 'When at his very best, Macfarlan was, from the Christian point of view, a dangerous character. The long battle of his life with fate, which never resulted in a single victory to him, soured his temper, made him a cynic; and when he spoke of Providence at all, he sneered at it.'[1] William Hodgson, who knew Macfarlan, reckoned that if he 'had been able to put his hand to his own plough — if, instead of looking for some social saviour, he had been his own — the probability is that he would have been to this hour an ornament and a power in the domain of letters. As it was he died, a victim of want of energy, while yet his magnificent gifts had hardly exercised themselves'.[2]

Occasional attempts were made at a more settled life. In 1857 Macfarlan called at the offices of the *Daily Bulletin*, run by Colin Rae-Brown, asking for employment as a court reporter. He supplied 'racy paragraphs' for a time until excuses became more frequent than copy, as Rae-Brown says in his Memoir of 1882, and he was dismissed. A few weeks later he sent the following autobiography with a note that read: 'What shall I say? What shall

1. 'Occasional Papers about Old Acquaintances. No. I. — James Macfarlan, Pedlar and Poet.' Newscutting pasted into copy of Macfarlan's works in the Glasgow Room of The Mitchell Library (Acc. no. 763715). A manuscript note attributes the article to William Hodgson writing in the *Fifeshire Journal*. The date must be early 1863.

2. *Ibid.*

Drygate 1849 from a painting by Thomas Fairbairn

I do? I am hopeless and penniless! Herewith you will receive the only promised autobiography of the most wretched and miserable of men, by name James Macfarlan.' Rae-Brown printed an edited version in his Memoir. This is the full version, insults and all, transcribed from the original manuscript, now in the Mitchell Library (Acc. no. 96566).

'SKETCH OF MY LIFE'

I was born in Glasgow 9th April 1832. My father who had been bred a weaver, had however previous to my birth given up his original calling for that of a pedlar, and I thus became a wanderer I may say from my infancy. Travelling from town to town it may be guessed, I could receive but little education, yet this wandering life although injurious to my progress in learning was in a manner favourable to poetic culture. By giving me an opportunity of visiting those scenes which have been celebrated in song or story, I had thus acquired a fund of sweet recollections which, in maturer years, were of great benefit in directing my thoughts to natural beauty. My mother, who was a delightful singer, very frequently chanted those old staves of love and chivalry which to my boyish fancy formed all that was desirable on earth, and filled my heart with a sense of melody which was to me strange and inexplicable. Happening to settle for a short time in Kilmarnock my parents placed me in a small academy of that town, where, after remaining for a short time, I acquired a slight English education, which with a few months schooling afterwards, in Glasgow, forms the whole amount of learning I ever received in a public manner. What little I have since gained has been the result of perseverance amid difficulties of the severest kind. When about 12 years of age, I was taken back to Glasgow where my father opened a small shop which he soon had to give up and recommenced his old trade of pedlar. In this occupation I joined him, and an odd volume of Byron's works which I found one day on a retired road let me to a love of reading. Books were now sought after wherever I could get them. By leaving a small deposit I borrowed books in almost every town where there was a public library, and my father who could rhyme a little himself, felt proud of my growing taste and encouraged me all he could. Thus did the time pass, and on reaching the age of 20 there was scarcely a standard work in the language which I had not perused. My thoughts were all along turned to poetry, and in 1853 having collected my scattered pieces together I determined on submitting them to the judgment of some person of critical ability, and accordingly,

I left my M.S. at the office of the Citizen newspaper addressed to the editor. The result was a long and flattering notice in the paper of the following Saturday, with copious extracts from my poems. Elated with this success, I resolved on publishing a volume by subscription, and after much difficulty — having walked all the way to and from London — succeeded in getting a London publisher to issue it. The volume was well noticed on its appearance in several respectable journals, but, coming out at a time when more experienced writers had engrossed the public attention, my less ambitious effort was soon forgotten, and many of my subscribers falling off, I was plunged into want and despair. In this state, I was very glad to accept a subordinate situation in the Glasgow Athenaeum, where I was engaged from nine in the morning, till half past ten at night. Tired of this, I again commenced travelling and peddling. About a year afterwards I returned to Glasgow, where my 'City Songs' were published and well received by the critics in general. Fortune however seemed to have set her face against me. From some cause which I never could learn I was discharged from more congenial employment which I had secured and, too sensitive to ask the reason I retired without making any questions. The world was now darkening around me. The consumptive tendencies of my constitution were beginning to develop themselves, and Death appeared to be rapidly approaching clad in that most fearful of all his garments — Want. Rendered, thus, desperate I wrote to the Earl of Carlisle to whom I had dedicated my last little work, stating my prospects, when his lordship returned me, through his secretary, the princely sum of one pound sterling!! Having about 200 copies of my book on hand, I resolved, as a means of recruiting my health, and gaining a livelihood, to go about selling them. I got a few circulars printed stating my circumstances, and the nature of my pursuits. With these I proceeded to Edinburgh where I met with but indifferent success. On an occasion of great embarrassment, I wrote to Mr Robert Chambers, imploring a little aid, and stating at the same time, my destitute condition. For three successive days did I call at that gentleman's office, but on no occasion had an answer been left. Almost exhausted with grief and suffering, suicide seemed to have become a necessity, and long and severe was the struggle before my better nature triumphed over the dark design of my crushed and trampled spirit. Returning to my native city, fresh trials awaited me. I commenced again to sell my little work and many and galling were the taunts to which I was subjected. 'Do you intend to live upon saw-dust and water? If not, burn your books and resign poetry.' Such was the insulting remark of a purse-proud gentleman who concluded his homily by pushing me out of his office. Such things had I to contend with till I became almost brokenhearted. Full of high hopes I called on the Rev. Norman Macleod author, of the 'Earnest Student' etc., in whom I hoped to find a patron. Timidly handing my little circular to the rev. gentleman, he threw it contemptuously back and slammed the door in my face. Tears gathered in my eyes as I departed from his princely residence, in the most fashionable part of the city, to my own miserable lodging in the purlieus of poverty 'where lonely want retires to die'. Burning with indignation I wrote the following letter which I was only withheld from sending by a strong effort.

Rev. Sir

A few nights ago I made bold to call on you in the hope that by making a small purchase of my poems you might throw me the means of providing my supper. I did not call, because you are a minister of the gospel, but because you are an author, which I hold to be something even higher. How you received me I leave your own heart to tell. I am poor Rev. Sir, but this day I would not exchange places with you for the crown of a Caesar. Burn this paper if you will, destroy it, but the words themselves are more deeply cut in the heart of the writer. They tell us that this is an age of scepticism, and who can wonder at it, when those who ought to be its strongest barriers offer the weakest points for the arrow of the unbeliever? And surely no one could recognise in such as the pompous and gold-bedizen'd Norman Macleod a follower of the meek and lowly Jesus!

James Macfarlan

This brings my life down to the present time when the waters of affliction are still around me. God knows what hand will come to snatch me out.

The despairing was a favourite mode for Macfarlan, but his talk of suicide was not entirely without foundation. Apparently he nearly became another 'body found': according to one account he went down to the Clyde at least five times intending to commit suicide, but, he said, had not the will.

As a result of his plea to Rae-Brown Macfarlan was employed on a freelance basis to supply 'legendary and other tales' for *The Workman*, the weekly version of the *Bulletin*. William Hodgson has left an account of his activities in this field: 'That he had the novelist's faculty, there never was any doubt, and that his pen was equal to an adequate, yea, powerful description of all sorts of scenes, there could be as little. Moreover, he had the art of putting the proper speeches into the mouths of the proper persons; that is to say, his lady or gentleman was always a lady or gentleman, and his hod-heaver always a hod-heaver; while, from his long intimacy with the lowest dens in the town, and with the lowest people in it, he was able, and he uniformly succeeded, in making them say just the very things they always said in their own style. In other words, all parties in his tales were completely idiomatic.'

Hodgson criticised him for what nowadays we should probably praise him: 'his constantly going to the Crescents and Sauchiehall Street for his villains, and supplying the real, genuine hero from the Wynds or the Goosedubs. The mischief was, as all his tales were Glasgow tales — manufactured, so to say, from home-made material — every one of his readers could judge of the utter unfairness of this as a social representation; and so as a storyteller he failed from the moral bias . . . which early, prolonged, and unpitying adversity had given his whole nature.'

He was a last-minute writer. 'The plot and the character . . . went simmering in his brain along the roadsides, in the lodging-houses, and, most of all, when sitting inspired in taverns. It was the very last day of the week, and almost uniformly the very last hour of it, before the "continued from our last" appeared.' He was an extremely erratic contributor and apologies were frequently printed for the 'illness' of the author. He used any paper that came to hand for his writing: 'tea paper, paper pocks, envelopes, or the very sweepings of country houses. . . . You could sometimes have traced their origin by their odour to some low den where the misery of the poor is heightened by the sickly smells of pigs' feet and hard ale. . . . We have Macfarlan's own words for saying that sometimes he wrote amid a very Babeldom of card playing, singing, quarrelling, drinking, and dancing.'[3]

Unfortunately we can hardly judge these stories as they do not seem to have survived. Two issues only of *The Workman* are extant, one (24 April 1858) containing 'The Passing Face: A Sketch' by 'Old Oliver'. Apparently Macfarlan contributed a column under the soubriquet 'Old Oliver in his Night Cap'. 'The Passing Face' is an ordinary enough piece, but holds interest for its early description of a brief encounter in a railway carriage. It was probably these sketches he refers to in a letter to Rae-Brown headed 6 April 1858, 144 King Street, Calton: 'the present tale in the "Workman" being near a close, I have entered on the composition of another entitled the 'Indian War-Path, or a Legend of the Wilds,' which from its name . . . will I think prove comparatively successful. In addition . . . I intend writing a light, racy sketch for each impression of the paper . . . I think under these circumstances, it may not be too impertinent to ask another shilling of advance on my present

3. *Ibid.*

weekly allowance, as I feel pretty tightly pressed at the moment.'

Macfarlan didn't stick at this, as he didn't stick at anything, going on the ran dan for months at a time, peddling his 'wee books', pestering folk to buy them — 'the birth and death of children', Rae-Brown comments, 'increasing his responsibilities, but failing to cure him of his rambling propensities.' He had married in 1855 Agnes Miller, a steam loom weaver from Belfast. She helped eke out their income by dressmaking.

As well as having various pamphlets printed Macfarlan contributed to Dickens's periodical *All the Year Round* from 1859 to 1861. In fact, this period would appear to hold a slight reversal of his misfortunes: regular publication in ATYR plus being taken up by *Tait's Edinburgh Magazine* (feature article, December 1858). He seems to have applied for the Secretaryship of the Glasgow Early Closing Association in 1861 — his letter of recommendation from Dickens still survives (Mitchell Library, MS.135/1). However, like most sallies in his life, these led to nothing.

Macfarlan took the pledge about 1860, but the damage had been done, after a lifetime of sleeping rough and drinking likewise. He is quoted as saying, 'Beggars canna be choosers, and when I feel a sinking within, whisky is surely better than naething'. The temperance missionary William Logan kept an eye on him, providing his family with some relief. The autumn of 1862 was particularly wet and Macfarlan's health grew worse. A friend paid for a medical examination: pulmonary consumption was diagnosed; the treatment recommended was warm clothing, fresh air and nourishing food. One can imagine a rare laugh from the poet.

On a cold October day he collapsed outside his house after a fruitless expedition trying to sell his pamphlet *The Attic Study*. 'He was put to bed and pronounced to be dying. . . . Warm bedclothes were brought to him and generous cordials administered: but it was all too late.'[4] According to one who visited him on his deathbed Macfarlan said he was sorry for the drink and now hated the smell of it. His last recorded utterance was, as his eye was caught by a blink of sun, 'Ah! there's heaven's sun — a glorious object; that sun is my Father's, and it is mine too, and I do enjoy it!' Self-dramatizing to the end! He died as the Cathedral bells chimed seven on 6 November 1862. He was buried in the Cheapside Street cemetery, Anderston. Fourteen poets and artists followed the coffin from the Drygate. It was an overcast, snowy day; as the body was lowered into the coffin there was a lightning flash and a peal of thunder.

4. A. C. Murdoch, *People's Friend* 2 June 1880, p. 339.

5. Obituary in *Glasgow Herald* 10 November 1862, 4e.

To his friends Macfarlan was an enigma, so it is not surprising how difficult it is now to get to grips with his character. A. G. Murdoch described his features as 'entirely destitute of intellectual character, and his manner diffident and slouching to the point of imbecility'.[6] To a visitor on his deathbed he had a 'fine symmetrical forehead, intelligent eye, and modest reserve'.[7] Rae-Brown wrote that he 'seemed to possess two separate and distinct individualities: one soaring high in the sunny empyrean of the sacred Nine, the other grovelling in the dingiest purlieus of the populous "City by the Clyde". Socially . . . he always remained at the very foot of the ladder of life. Physically, he was one of the poorest specimens of our common humanity. Predisposed to consumption, wan and dejected of visage, always meanly clad, and continually craving "assistance", he generally got a "wide berth" in the daylight.' William Hodgson wrote that he 'was extremely unpresentable. There never was such a great mind in such a vile body. He seemed to have suffered at some railway collision, and went huddled up as if conserving his contusions.'[8] George Eyre-Todd described his appearance thus: 'About five feet six in height, always meanly clad, with heavy commonplace features, sallow, fair complexion, and dull brown eyes, he wore a browbeaten, dejected look.'[9] No portrait of him has so far been found — it is doubtful if one was ever made.

He made a way of life from constant rebuffs, inviting the wide berth. Those who offered to help him — and he did have several friends, Rae-Brown, William Logan, James P. Crawford and W. T. McAuslane among them — were often sorely tried by his attitude — he bit all hands:

> Friends I have had — not many. Who they were
> It matters not — enough that they are some:
> All fair and false, and falsest when most fair
> ('A November Night Piece')

As Richard Ellmann said of James Joyce, he was 'not a man to be helped with impunity'. Eyre-Todd wrote that Macfarlan 'scorned honest labour, sneered at honour and gratitude as mere cant, and scrupled no whit to swindle and beg'. He also tells of the night Macfarlan knocked up the poet David Gray, asking for assistance as one of his children had died. Gray had no

6. A. C. Murdoch, *op. cit.*

7. *Glasgow Herald* 10 November 1862, 4e.

8. William Hodgson, *op. cit.*

9 George Eyre-Todd, *The Glasgow Poets* (Glasgow and Edinburgh: William Hodge, 1903), p. 181.

money, which was just as well — the story was a pack of lies. And there is a letter (now in the Mitchell Library) dated 1859 from the English poet Gerald Massey to Macfarlan, thanking him for his 'pleasant volume' and protesting at Macfarlan calling Fame fickle: 'If you are a Poet, be sure Fame will find it out.' Macfarlan's friend J. P. Crawford has scribbled on it: 'Sold to me by Macfarlan for a 6d. to Buy drink no doubt'.

And what about the poems themselves? Contemporary writers tended to concentrate, predictably, on what-might-have-been, on the genius cut down before realising his potential — and there are hints that he might have developed, though more as a prose writer, in the way that Alexander Smith did (fiction, essays, etc.). In truth, most of Macfarlan's poetry, considered apart from his life, is fairly run-of-the-mill stuff, the writing of a young man steeped in Keats and Shelley and in love with POESY.

Insofar as Macfarlan fits in anywhere, he would seem to belong to the group of self-taught poets termed 'The Parnassians' by Brian Maidment in his study, *The Poorhouse Fugitives* (1987). These poets did not write in dialect nor did they appear to be influenced by contemporary politics. They had, as Maidment puts it, 'a sense of the poet as an anguished, lonely and solitary figure, oppressed by the moral and social failings of a wicked world'.[11] He further defines the poet of this school as one who 'might be seen as merely an exaggerating of the Romantic poet, questing in solitude for spirituality, for meaning, and for identity through hopelessly large claims for poetry as a social and moral force. Poetry by self-taught ambitious writers might be read not entirely as a cultural gesture on behalf of the aspiring artisans, but rather as a desperate quest for an individual sense of coherence and purpose among the earliest and most spectacular casualties of urban industrialisation, differing from the Romantics not so much in aim or kind but rather in the more precise location of their alienation in the industrial experience of Manchester, Sheffield, or Leeds.' Or Glasgow.

Their subjects were the city versus the country, Nature, innocence and childhood — the staples, in fact, of Macfarlan's poetry, the city being felt particularly oppressive:

> pent in this vile city
>> ('Light and Darkness')
> The city where wide-throated chimneys pour
> Their black foul breath upon the blue of heaven
>> ('Summer')

10. *Ibid.*

11. Brian Maidment, *The Poorhouse Fugitives: Self-taught poets and poetry in Victorian Britain* (Manchester: Carcanet Press, 1987), p. 98.

and see also his *City Songs* (1855). Martha Vicinus's comments, 'They [Parnassian-type poets] endorsed the Romantic conception of the poet. Alienated from every class, they promoted their own special poetic sensibility,'[12] might have been written with Macfarlan in mind instead of the English poets, including Joseph Skipsey and John Nicholson, she was discussing. The life of Nicholson (1790-1843) offers a parallel to Macfarlan's: 'a series of short-lived jobs, repeated requests for money from sympathisers, and finally escape through alcoholism'.[13]

When Macfarlan stops waffling about Nature and Poesy he can write stirring stuff, like 'The Lords of Labour' (praised by Thackeray) or 'A Hymn of Hope' — composed in what the *Dictionary of National Biography* calls 'fluent and resonant English'. Hope, it soon becomes obvious, is the principal leitmotif of Macfarlan's life and work — a continual hoping against hope, contributing to what one critic described as the 'strain of helpless melancholy' that runs through his poetry:

Hope in my heart is queen
 ('Light and Darkness')

Like hope! ah, wherefore cheat the heart?
 ('Maid Margery')

Hope shall wake on that glorious morn
 ('Harvest Home')

brood o'er beauty and the hopes of youth
 ('Pictures of the Past')

The Romantic influence has been mentioned; a perhaps to us more interesting influence on Macfarlan was Edgar Allan Poe. Edwin Morgan has drawn attention to the 'Poe-like vision' of Macfarlan's poem 'The Ruined City' and other echoes of Poe can be discerned, particularly of his 'time-eaten towers' (cf. Macfarlan's 'the mouldering tower of Time'). Morgan has aptly summed up Macfarlan's importance: he 'used all his miseries to project something general and almost mythical about the individual, and especially the creative individual, in industrial society.[14] This is exemplified in his long poem 'The Wanderer' (usually referred to as 'The Wanderer of the West'; the only contemporary copy seen, that of the second edition, is titled 'The

12. Martha Vicinus, *The Industrial Muse* (Croom Helm, 1974), p. 144.

13. *Ibid.*

14. Edwin Morgan, 'Scottish Poetry in the Nineteenth Century' in *The History of Scottish Literature* vol. 3, ed. Douglas Gifford (Aberdeen: Aberdeen University Press, 1988), p. 342.

Wanderer') about a youthful poet struggling to escape from 'the dungeon floor of poverty'. Like Alexander Smith's poem 'Glasgow' it contains some memorable urban images:

> Mighty furnaces are flaring like a demon's breath of fire,
> Forges, like burning cities, break in many a crimson spire

or others, like the poet 'Moleing for ever the golden-sanded soil'.

Forever trying to escape the city (to the country of his childhood) Macfarlan nonetheless is a poet of the city, of its 'jarring life' as he called it. He experienced most keenly there the transience of things and people: 'cities crumble down / And sleep in their own dust' ('Light and Darkness'). He is very much a voice from the city, occasionally even Baudelaire-like in his alone-ness in the teeming metropolis:

> I stood at noontide 'mid the flood-like throng,
> Pouring incessant through the city street
> ('Written in the City')

This is necessarily a brief introduction to Macfarlan. There is still a lot to be done: on his biography, on tracking down his scattered poems, on exploring issues such as the relationship of his poems to those of Alexander Smith (there have been charges of plagiarism),[15] and on an examination of his work in general and his place in 19th century literature — he was such an archetypical romantic poet (consumption, garret, early death) that, if for nothing else, he deserves rediscovery. In Edwin Morgan's poem 'Rider' — a surrealistic piece about Glasgow poets past and present — Macfarlan finds a place — and a fitting epitaph:

> James Macfarlan threw his pen at the stinking wall/the whisky and the stinking
>   poverty
> ran down like ink/the well of rats was bottomless and Scotch/the conman and the
>   conned
> fought on/the ballads yellowed, the pubs filled/at Anderston he reached his grave
>   in snow/selah
> the ruined cities were switched off/there was no flood/his father led a pedlar's
>   horse
> by Carrick fields, his mother sang/the boy rode on a jogging back/far back/in
>   rags/
> Dixon's Blazes roared and threw more poets in its molten pools/forges on fire
> matched the pitiless bread, the head
> long hangdog, the lifted elbow/
> the true bloody pathos and sublime

15. See Robert Crawford, 'Alexander Smith, James Macfarlan, and City Poetry'. *Scottish Literary Journal* 12:2, November 1985, pp. 35-52.

Appendix I

WORKS by James Macfarlan

Poems. London: Robert Hardwicke, 1854.
City Songs and Other Poetical Pieces. Glasgow: Thomas Murray, 1855.
Lyrics of Life. London: D. Bogue, 1856. (Includes 'Sketch of the Author's Life' by A.A.)
The Wanderer: A Poem. Glasgow: Thomas Murray and London: Arthur Hall; Virtue & Co., [1857?]. (Two editions.)
Poems. Glasgow: Printed by Thomas King, 1860.
Poems Contributed to 'All the Year Round'. Glasgow: Printed by J. Wright, [1861?].
The Attic Study: Brief Notes on Nature, Men and Books. Glasgow: Hugh Baird, 1862.
The Poetical Works. With a memoir by Colin Rae-Brown. Glasgow: Robert Forrester, 1882.

Rae-Brown's edition of the Poetical Works contains all of Macfarlan's poems previously published in book or pamphlet form, except the dramatic sketch 'Light and Darkness' from *Poems* (1854), plus some from manuscript sources and from periodicals. There are still some uncollected poems, for example: 'Night in the Sick-Room' (*Tait's Edinburgh Magazine* December 1858), 'Sir Faulchion' (*Tait's* March 1959), 'The Roadside Inn: Epistle' and 'The Two Paths' (*Tait's* May 1859). Three prose pieces, 'Wayside Thoughts', were published posthumously in *Hedderwick's Miscellany*, 29 November 1862, 13 December 1862, 14 February 1863.

The Mitchell Library holds a few manuscripts by Macfarlan: those used by Rae-Brown for his edition (the 'Sketch of My Life', 15 poems and a letter, 1858, to Rae-Brown — Acc. no. 96566) and a version of 'The Rhymer' (pasted into a presentation copy to Alexander Smith of *Poems*, 1854, along with a letter, 1859, to Macfarlan, from Gerald Massey — Acc. no. 763716).

Appendix II

SOME POEMS by James Macfarlan

SUNLIGHT IN THE LANE

I live amid the roar of streets,
The never-ending tide that beats
   On lofty dwellings dun;
For years my only joy has been
To watch the fluctuating scene
   Beneath the clouded sun.

O many a dreary year is past
Since I beheld the ocean last,
   Or heard the forest choirs;
Since last I trod the heather dell.
Ere I had come alone to dwell,
   Amid the clanging spires.

The music of the mountain stream
Is like a dim dissolving dream
   Within a waking brain;
I hear the brawling of the brooks
From which the pictured forest looks,
   And I am young again.

I could not think to dwell alone
Amid this endless monotone.
   And nurse Self's barren brood,
Without some joy my soul to fill.
Teaching me in this sea of ill
   To find some pearls of good.

In dingy court, or alley dim,
The linnet's sweet and day-long hymn,
   To me a pleasure yields;
And, in the sultry summer hours,
A dusty knot of fingered flowers,
   Recalls the breezy fields.

A tuft of dull down-trodden grass,
In some still by-way where I pass,
    Brings summer to my heart;
And visions of blue violet plots,
White daisies, and forget-me-nots,
    Will from the pathway start.

The passing faces on the street,
The kindly talk when kindred meet,
    Have been a joy to me;
And though in crowds I dwell alone,
My heart has long familiar grown
    With all I hear and see.

And in the long dull dripping days.
When ne'er a gleam of sunshine strays
    Along the rainy roofs,
I hear, in some old song of arms,
The knightly frays, the loud alarms,
    The rush of ringing hoofs.

Thus, in the fairy realms of rhyme
My heart has found a golden clime
    With many a sylvan store,
Of flowery cup, and trembling bell,
And leaning boughs, where warblers tell
    Of summer's leafy lore.

O let me still such day-dreams share,
Or, dwelling mid these caves of care,
    My toiling heart will break;
O let me hope that Love still brings
Some goodness from the meanest things
    For sovereign Beauty's sake!

(*City Songs*, 1855)

THE MIDNIGHT TRAIN

Across the dull and brooding night,
A giant flies with demon light,
   And breath of wreathing smoke;
Around him whirls the reeling plain,
And, with a dash of grim disdain,
   He cleaves the sundered rock.

In lonely swamps the low wind stirs
The belt of black funereal firs,
   That murmur to the sky,
Till, startled by his mad career,
They seem to keep a hush of fear,
   As if a god swept by!

Through many a dark wild heart of heath,
O'er booming bridges, where beneath
   A midnight river brawls;
By ruin, remnants of the past,
Their ivies trembling in the blast;
   By singing waterfalls!

The slumb'rer on his silent bed,
Turns to the light his lonely head,
   Divested of its dream.
Long leagues of gloom are hurried o'er,
Through tunnel-sheaths, with iron roar,
   And shrill night-rending scream.

Past huddling huts, past flying farms,
High furnace flames, whose crimson arms
   Are grappling with the night,
He tears along receding lands,
To where the kingly city stands,
   Wrapt in a robe of light.

Here, round each wide and gushing gate,
A crowd of eager faces wait,
   And every smile is known.
We thank thee, O thou Titan train,
That in the city once again,
   We clasp our loved, our own!

(*All the Year Round* 3 December 1859)

THE LORDS OF LABOUR

They come, they come, in a glorious march!
    You can hear their steam-steeds neigh,
As they dash through Skill's triumphal arch,
    Or plunge 'mid the dancing spray.
Their bale-fires blaze in the mighty forge,
    Their life-pulse throbs in the mill,
Their lightnings shiver the gaping gorge,
    And their thunders shake the hill.
Ho! these are the Titans of toil and trade,
    The heroes who wield no sabre;
But mightier conquests reapeth the blade
    That is borne by the Lords of Labour.

Brave hearts, like jewels, light the sod,
    Through the mists of commerce shine;
And souls flash out, like stars of God,
    From the midnight of the mine.
No palace is theirs, no castle great,
    No princely, pillared hall;
But they well can laugh at the roofs of state,
    'Neath the heaven which is over all.
Ho! these are Titans of toil and trade,
    The heroes who wield no sabre;
But mightier conquests reapeth the blade
    That is borne by the Lords of Labour!

Each bares his arm for the ringing strife
    That marshals the sons of the soil;
And the sweat-drops shed in their battle of life
    Are gems in the crown of Toil.
And prouder their well-won wreaths, I trow,
    Than laurels with life-blood wet;
And nobler the arch of a bare bold brow,
    Than the clasp of a coronet.
Then hurrah for each hero, although his deed
    Be unblown by the trump or tabor;
For holier, happier far, is the meed
    That crowneth the Lords of Labour.

(*Poems*, 1860)

THE RUINED CITY

The shadows of a thousand springs,
    Unnumbered sunsets, sternly sleep
Above the dust of perished things
    That form this city's blasted heap.
Dull watch the crumbling columns keep
    Against the fierce relentless sky,
Hours, that no dial noteth, creep
    Like unremembered phantoms by;
And still this city of the dead,
Gives echo to no human tread.

A curse is writ on every stone,
    The Temple's latest pillar, lies
Like some white Mammoth's bleaching bone,
    Its altars know no deities.
Fine columns of a palace-rise,
    And when the sun is red and low,
And glaring in the molten skies,
    A shadow huge these columns throw,
That like some dark colossal hand
In silence creeps across the sand.

The Senate slumbers, wondrous hive
    Of councils sage, of subtle schemes;
But does no lingering tone survive
    To prove their presence more than dreams?
No light of revelation beams
    Around that voiceless Forum now,
Time bears upon his restless streams
    No reflex of the haughty brow
That oft has frowned a nation's fate
Here — where dark reptiles congregate.

Where, where is now the regal rag
    That clothed the monarch of yon tower,
On which the rank weed flaps its flag
    Across the dusk this sombre hour?
Alas! for pomp, alas! for power,
    When time unveils their nakedness.
And Valour's strength and Beauty's flower
    Find nought to echo their distress;
And flattery — fine delusive breath
    Melts in the iron grasp of Death.

Day rises with an angry glance,
  As if to blight the stagnant air.
And hurls his fierce and fiery lance
  On that Doomed City's forehead bare.
The sunset's wild and wandering hair
  Streams backward like a comet's mane,
And from the deep and sullen glare
  The shuddering columns crouch in vain,
And through the wreck of wrathful years
  The grim hyaena stalks and sneers.

(*All the Year Round* 7 January 1860)

A MAN OF FEELING

O much he talked and much he wrote,
　　Fine words of feeling, nicely blent
With tender touches, sweet to quote,
　　And little thrills of sentiment.

O fine and sympathetic toes
　　That turned aside to spare the worm,
Kind heart, that disregarded woes
　　Which merely took a human form.

Except when far Tahiti's sons
　　Could draw his bounty o'er the main,
And leave those hungry wretched ones
　　To perish in a neighbouring lane.

O noble soul! surpassing all
　　In depth of pity, breadth of sense.
How often has the crowded hall
　　Re-echoed to thine eloquence.

And men bepraised the liberal hand,
　　And men extoled the mighty views,
And spread the name throughout the land
　　That figured in the morning news.

Then reverence the good man's grave,
　　And let your grief be like his own,
And give him all *he* ever gave
　　That soft and tender thing — a stone!

[*c*. 1862]

PUBLICATIONS BY JOE FISHER

Dunlops of Garnkirk and Tollcross Papers: A Catalogue. Glasgow Room, 1971. (Typescript).

T. Annan's Old Closes and Streets of Glasgow: a guide. Glasgow: Mitchell Library, 1977. (Typescript).

St. John Ogilvie S.J. 1579-1615: An illustrated history of his life, martyrdom and canonisation. Glasgow: Third Eye Centre, 1979. Contributed essays: 'Scotland, Trials and Martyrdom' (pp. 11-15) and 'Glasgow in John Ogilvie's Time' (pp. 51-54).

Glasgow Newspapers 1715-1979: A chronological guide. Glasgow Room, 1979. (typescript).

Helen Bell, *John Maclean: a selected bibliography.* With an introduction by Joseph A. Fisher. Glasgow: Glasgow Collection, Mitchell Library, 1980. (Typescript).

Derek Smith and J. A. Fisher, *Thomas Annan, Photographer of Glasgow, 1868-1877.* Glasgow: Third Eye Centre, 1981. (Exhibition brochure).

Oscar Marzaroli, *Shades of Grey: Glasgow 1956-1987.* Photographs by Oscar Marzaroli. Words by William McIlvanney. Notes by Joe Fisher and Cordelia Oliver. Edinburgh: Mainstream, in conjunction with Third Eye Centre, 1987.

Auld Hawkie and Other Glasgow Characters. Drawn by Dorothy Whitaker. Poems by Freddie Anderson. Text by Joe Fisher, Glasgow: Glasgow District Libraries, 1988.

CONTRIBUTIONS TO PERIODICALS:

LOCSCOT
'People's History: the Voice of the Working Class'. 1:1, Winter 1981, pp. 17-19.
'Local Studies Publications: Deposit Collection'. 1:3, Autumn 1982, p. 53.
'Local Studies Publications: Deposit Collection'. 1:5, Autumn 1983, p. 87.
'Membership Survey'. 1:6, Spring 1984, pp. 110-1.
'Local Studies Publications: Deposit Collection'. 1:7, Autumn 1984, p. 135.
'Chairman's Report'. 1:8, Spring 1985, p. 144.
'Chairman's Report'. 1:9, Autumn 1985, p. 164.
'Chairman's Report'; review of *Lennox Links*. 1:10, Spring 1986, pp. 184, 196.
'Chairman's Report'. 1:11, Autumn 1986, p. 204.
'Chairman's Report'. 2:2, Winter 1987, p. 2.
'Resources for Burgh History'. 2:3, Summer 1988, pp. 1-2.
'Chairman's Report'. 2:4, Winter 1988, pp. 2-3.
'Chairman's Report'. 2:5, Spring 1989, p. 3.
'Chairman's Report'. 2:6, Winter 1989, p. 3.
'Chairman's Report'. 2:7, Spring 1990, p. 3.

THE SCOTTISH POST (Journal of Scottish Postal History Society)
'The Post'. No. 24, October-December 1984.